AF584395

NONNA KNOWS BEST

NONNA KNOWS BEST

THE ITALIAN ART OF LIVING WELL

JACLYN CRUPI

Jaclyn Crupi

Jaclyn Crupi is a bookseller at Hill of Content Bookshop in Melbourne and a freelance book editor and project manager. She has written numerous children's books ranging from board books for babies to fiction for middle graders to craft kits for tweens and teens.

Jaclyn has worked in publishing and bookselling since 2002. She has a Bachelor of Arts from Melbourne University and a Graduate Diploma in Editing and Publishing from RMIT. She has contributed book reviews to *Slow Magazine* and *The Lifted Brow* and is a regular bookstagrammer.

When Jaclyn isn't reading or editing you will find her in her garden or kitchen. The tradition of tomato day continues each year.

Felicita Sala

Felicita is a self-taught illustrator. She was born in Rome but grew up in Perth, where she graduated in Philosophy from the University of Western Australia.

One of her books was selected among the 10 best illustrated books by the *New York Times* in 2018. She has worked on papercut animations for music videos and made illustrated recipes for magazines, but her passion is making picture books for children.

She lives in Rome with her husband Gianluca and their daughter Nina.

~

For Nonna Paolina and Nonna Vincenzina,
if you know me, you know them

75

X4J
FZL

Introduction

Chapter one: Mangia e bevi

Chapter two: La filosofia di nonna

Chapter three: Amore e famiglia

CONTENTS

Live life nonna style

There is nothing better than having a nonna and I should know: I had two of them. A nonna will love you unconditionally, feed you continuously and guide you through life with passion and passata. My nonnas taught me everything I needed to know about life, love and family, and I remain convinced that the nonna way of life is the best way of life. Each nonna is different, of course, but their approach to life is rooted in the same philosophy: live a vibrant life, celebrate what you have, cherish family and make sugo.

If you want life to have more pleasure, more joy, more excitement, more community, more delicious food and more wild gesticulating, then you need only look to the nonnas. They really do know best. If you're looking for an approach to life that will ensure it is pleasure-filled, joyous and bold then read on to follow the way of the nonnas. I'll be telling stories of my own nonnas throughout this book as well as those of the friends I spoke to about their nonnas. The wit and wisdom of these women is hard to contain in a book this small but hopefully their bold and joyous personalities will jump off the page and come to full-scale nonna life. These women shaped us, they cared for us, they showed us what love looks like and they made us the people we are.

There is nothing minimal or restrained about a nonna. A nonna comes at you full throttle while at the same time knowing that the best way to follow a huge meal is with a nice nap. She wants life to be full and rich and colourful. Nonnas will never tell you to downsize, clear out, simplify. They want you to take giant gulps of life. Eat carbs. Drink wine. This life of ours is short so you need to live big – nonna style.

A nonna is the only person who, when you show up unannounced, will open the door pulling a pizza out of the oven as she 'had a feeling' you might stop by. A nonna's sixth sense cannot be denied. Or perhaps she just makes pizza every day in case you do visit. Either way, there is no better way to welcome a person than with homemade pizza. And nobody shows love through food better than a nonna.

A nonna's love could power the country. She shows us how big love can be. Love is shown through food, of course, but also through hugs that leave you breathless, a willingness to help you with anything you may need, a deep understanding of who you are and a tiny sprinkling of guilt. They just can't help themselves.

Don't be fooled though – Nonnas aren't just pure love. They are also ruthless and cunning, ready to strike at a moment's notice. Play Italian card games with them and they will reveal this side of themselves immediately. A nonna will not let you win. She will not encourage you if you do well. She will destroy you. *Briscola, scopa* or the aptly named *bestia* will bring this to the fore, and the glint in her eyes as she crushes you at cards will chill you to your core. All will be forgotten over a coffee and biscotto. But never forget, Nonna plays to win and she is not mucking around.

Nonnas work hard and they play hard. Life is lived to the full. They are never too tired to cook and there is no such thing as takeaway (see page 69). There is always time for one more coffee. Pasta is handmade (it's much easier than you think plus it's good chatting and singing time). Babies cheeks aren't going to squeeze themselves.

Italy is ranked as one of the healthiest countries on earth by the Bloomberg Global Health Index. A baby born in Italy today can expect to live to be an octogenarian (i.e. a nonna or nonno). There's definitely something to be said for the Italian lifestyle and Mediterranean diet. These nonnas enjoy long, healthy lives (*se Dio vuole*/God willing) and there is so much you can learn from them. How to be happy. How to be healthy. What a good long life can look like. Many nonnas attribute their health to the olive oil they cook with, drink four tablespoons of per day and rub on their skin. Many say it's their families and grandchildren who keep them young. And some simply raise their hands and say, 'Boh!'. Nonnas are national treasures and whatever explains their longevity we welcome it with open arms and well-pinched cheeks.

It's worth mentioning that any nonna found outside Italy was brave and bold enough to move to another country. She was probably young when she did this. She may not have spoken the language of the country she moved to. She might have had small children. The journey might have been long and difficult. Finding herself in a new and very different country from the one she came from may have been incredibly challenging. But she did it. She rose to meet the opportunity the new country offered her and her family. She helped her family thrive. She set them and future generations up for success. She did it all with love and laughter, because that's what nonnas do – they hold up the sky.

So if you're looking for an approach to life that will ensure it is rich in meaning, joyous and bold then follow the way of the nonnas. They will not lead you astray (unless you're playing cards and then you can't say we didn't warn you). If you can embrace life half as well as nonnas, you'll be very lucky. If you can learn to appreciate the handmade, the passionate, the emotional, the bold, the loving, you'll be better for it. Nonnas to the front!

HOW MUCH NONNA POTENTIAL DO YOU HAVE?

So you've seen the light and want to live the most nonna-esque life possible. Take this quiz so you can assess your nonna potential.

1. A friend has dropped in. Do you:

a. Brew espresso and get out the deck of cards

b. Suggest you go for a walk around the neighbourhood

c. Drag them into the garden and pick a bag of lemons for them to take home

d. All of the above

2. The sun is shining through the window. Do you:

a. Grab your car keys and drive to the beach

b. Pick up a shammy – that window is filthy

c. Start to write a to-do list of all the jobs you need to get done

d. Stare outside and let your mind empty while enjoying the simplicity and beauty of the moment

3. Your family is coming for lunch. Do you:

a. Order Uber Eats

b. Book a table at your local restaurant

c. Rustle together a simple lunch from what you have in the fridge

d. Start cooking a multi-course meal

4. What oil do you have in your house?

a. Rice bran oil

b. Coconut oil

c. Peanut oil

d. Olive oil

5. You're playing cards with a young child. Do you:

a. Let them cheat

b. 'Accidentally' show your cards to help them out

c. You would never play cards with a child

d. Ruthlessly and without hesitation beat them

Mostly As

You're lovely, and you have some nonna tendencies but you're not yet a full-blown nonna. Read on and pay particular attention to the chapters on *dolce far niente* and food and drink.

Mostly Bs

You're lovely, and you have some nonna tendencies but you're not yet a full-blown nonna. Read on and pay particular attention to the chapters on food and drink and the philosophies of being a nonna.

Mostly Cs

You're lovely, and you have some nonna tendencies but you're not yet a full-blown nonna. Read on and pay particular attention to the chapters on *dolce far niente* and food and drink.

Mostly Ds

You are the truest nonna who has ever lived. You don't even need this book, though I suspect you will enjoy it and relate to it. The nonna in you is strong. Get back to your passata.

GETTING IN TOUCH WITH YOUR INNER NONNA

Here are some quick and easy ways to get in touch with your inner nonna.

Play cards aggressively and delight in your victories.

~

Talk with your hands, gesticulating wildly (see page 252 for a visual guide to Italian hand gestures).

~

Throw salt over your left shoulder.

~

Cook an incredible meal from ingredients you have grown in your garden and start apologising for it as soon as you serve it to your guests.

~

Fill your pantry with homemade preserves.

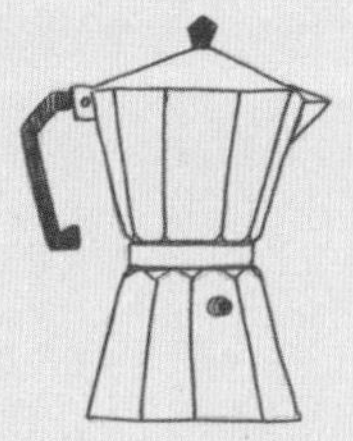

Put the *caffettiera* (Italian coffee pot) on and let the smell transport you to any nonna's house.

~

Wear a housedress with an apron over the top at all times when at home.

~

Pinch the cheeks of babies and small children.

~

Give advice passionately and then raise your hands and shrug your shoulders as if to say, 'But what do I know.'

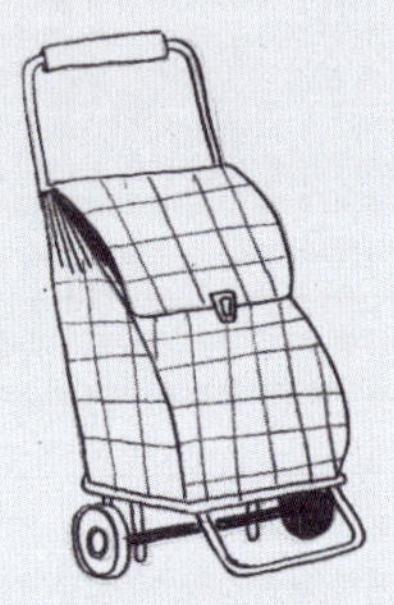

THE 5 ESSENTIAL THINGS YOU NEED TO GET IN TOUCH WITH YOUR INNER NONNA

1. Invest in a house dress or dedicate an old dress to be a house dress. Extra points if it's paisley or floral.

2. Get a striped or floral apron and wear it whenever you cook or whenever you have aforementioned house dress on.

3. If you want to get serious about cooking like a nonna, get a *passa tutto* (vegetable mill), a pasta machine and a *caffettiera* – you need not buy these things new, go to op shops as they are commonly found there.

4. You need a trolley to do your shopping if you truly want to embrace the nonna approach to life. It will save your arms when you inevitably end up buying more than you intended.

5. A deck of Italian cards is essential to live life like a nonna.

CETRIOLI
ITALIA
€ 2,80/kg

PEPERONI
NUMERO BILANCIA
ITALIA
CALIBRO
/Kg.
NUMERO
CALIBRO
550

olio
extra

CHAPTER ONE

~

MANGIA E BEVI

Food is love

For Italian nonnas, the greatest expression of love is through food. 'Mangia, mangia' – meaning 'eat, eat' – might be the most repeated phrase in all of Italy. If a nonna had her way she would feed her family continuously. By feeding you, she can show you how much she loves you, how much she wants to nurture you, how important you are. Nonnas may not be overly sentimental but they make up for it as aggressive food pushers, all in the name of love.

Consider how beloved Italian food is all around the world. It's beloved for a reason – nonnas are the best cooks and have set the standard for how delicious and nutritious food should be. We have doctors and nutritionists around the world telling us that not only is the *Italian* diet* the healthiest way to eat, but that they also now think it makes us live longer.

* Well, okay, they didn't specify the Italian diet. They said the *Mediterranean* diet, which, strictly speaking, includes Greece and other countries bordering the Mediterranean Sea. But this book isn't called *Yiayia Knows Best*! So, if you want to embrace the way of the nonnas, step one is a deep love and appreciation for food, where it comes from and how it's cooked.

Mangia! Mangia!

Many nonnas take great pride in their cooking. Nothing gives them more joy than seeing their family and friends enjoying their food. And nothing makes them more unhappy than the phrase 'Thanks, but I'm full.' It must be stressed: you *have* to eat … and eat and eat and eat. A nonna will notice exactly what you put in your mouth, how many serves you have and what foods you avoid. She will remember every morsel. Paying attention to what you eat is part of the meal for any nonna – in fact, it's almost a sport. A nonna will show her love by giving you food, and you must return that love by eating and enjoying it (it's not hard). What could be more beautiful, symbiotic and powerful than that!

Enjoy seeing people eat the food you have made them. Try to hear the compliments they offer. Cooking and eating need to be seen as the acts of love that they are.

Slow food

Food is not to be rushed. Nonnas often grow their own seasonal produce, and they love tending to their gardens. They pick their produce when it's at its absolute peak and then either cook it while it's fresh, or preserve, pickle, freeze, air-dry or ferment it. Some people put money in the bank, nonnas put it in the *cantina* (pantry or cellar). Nonnas do not rely on processed foods – they make their own pasta, they mince their own meat, they grow and shell their own peas. The time and effort nonnas devote to food is all about love. It represents their love of good honest food and their desire to nourish their nearest and dearest (and strangers as well – nonnas just want to feed people).

Take the time to think about where your food comes from and always buy the best-quality ingredients you can afford. If you truly want to embrace an Italian way of life, food will become central to your being and any nonna would be very proud of you.

Simplicity perfected

Italian flavours are bold and surprisingly simple. You will not find any molecular desserts or tweezered micro greens on a nonna's table. Nonna's food is hearty, it's simple and the flavour always packs a knockout punch. Think prosciutto and melon; tomatoes and basil; coffee and mascarpone, and bread and the greenest, freshest olive oil you have ever seen. Nonnas do not mess around with flavour. They are not going for subtlety or complexity. They want you groaning in pleasure with each mouthful. Food is to be devoured and not a drop or crumb should go to waste. Once you've eaten a huge bowl of pasta, there is bread for *scarpetta* (mopping up the sauce on your plate).

There is beauty in the simplicity, but there is also nowhere to hide. Every ingredient needs to be perfect or the meal won't sing. Nonnas don't cut corners when it comes to food. So take the time to make bread, to hand-roll pasta, to macerate strawberries in sugar and orange juice, to shell broad beans (twice!) and to grind coffee beans fresh for each brew. Bring simplicity back into your life. Meals do not need to be complicated to be incredible.

Meals at the table

You will not find nonnas eating dinner on their laps or standing up at the kitchen bench. Meals are served at the table, always. This is non-negotiable. The television might be on, in fact it probably will be, but nobody will be able to hear it over the loud conversation. Food will arrive and the table will groan under the weight of it. Some dishes such as lasagna will be plated in the kitchen, others will be placed on the table in large serving platters. Nonna will know what your favourite meals are and she will make them for you regularly. Remember: food is love. Sitting at the table to eat is an Italian way of life and it simply wouldn't occur to most Italians to do it any differently. It's a way of celebrating the delicious food being served and the family time together. Don't have meals on the run, take the time to sit and appreciate the food you are eating and the people you are eating it with. Food might sustain us, but the love of food nurtures us. Start to love your food and it will become so natural to you that you wouldn't want to rush the experience of enjoying it.

Love food

In Italy, lunch is often the biggest meal of the day and traditionally all family members return home from school or work for lunch. Having the biggest meal in the middle of the day means you get to burn off some of the calories, rather than eating a large meal and then going to bed soon after. Italians would argue that it's not always *what* you eat but *when* you eat. No nonna is going to serve you a sandwich for lunch (or dinner for that matter). Meals are not eaten quickly at a desk. Appreciating the role of food and meals in your life is a way to bring joy and appreciation to your table and home. Food is not just about sustenance, it's also about love. Love the food you make, love the food you eat, love the people you cook for – Nonna wouldn't have it any other way. *Buon appetito*!

TALES OF NONNA

'I had been seeing my non-Italian (scandaloso) *boyfriend for a few months when I decided it was about time he met my nonna. We arranged a Sunday lunch and I explained to my boyfriend that all he really needed to do was eat my nonna's delicious food … and tell her repeatedly how delicious is was. On the big day, after an antipasto, Nonna brought out plates of homemade lasagna; steaming hot, crispy on the outside, soft on the inside, just how I like it. We ate.'*

'She asked my boyfriend if he'd like more and he said yes. She brought another huge serve, which he quickly ate. She offered thirds and he agreed. I was surprised by how much he was eating but Nonna was so happy and she clearly liked this guy. He declined a fourth serve of lasagna and we cleared the plates. Nonna and I returned to the table with the main course: roast beef, roast potatoes, peas, cotolette, arancini and a salad. My boyfriend looked at the food perplexed. He thought the meal was over, not realising the lasagna was just the entrée. Such a rookie mistake.' – J

But first, coffee

Coffee is, without a doubt, the source of a nonna's seemingly endless supply of energy. Nonnas cannot be expected to function without this black, liquid magic. It gives them their bustle and their spark. Be like nonna – drink coffee.

Coffee is an important part of life in Italy. According to coffee-research institutions, roughly fourteen billion espressos are consumed each year in Italy, and most of this coffee is consumed at home (despite there being about 120,000 coffee bars in Italy). For many Italians, a house without a *caffettiera* is simply not a place people should be expected to live. The *caffettiera* is to the Italian kitchen what the kettle is to the British. And just as tea is an integral part of British culture, coffee is the lifeblood of Italy – a life without coffee is unimaginable. An espresso will get your heart racing and your body moving – basically it's a jumpstart in a tiny cup. It's worth knowing how Italian coffee culture works and taking from it what works best for you.

Standing at the bar

If you're travelling in Italy and want to drink coffee like a real Italian nonna, you should prop yourself at the bar with the locals. For a small premium you could take a seat at a table. Italian nonnas don't spend a lot of time in cafes drinking coffee. They simply sip their espresso and are on their way. In Italy a coffee break is known as *una pausa* (a pause) and that is quite literally all it is: a pause in the day. A nonna might have four or five pauses per day but they'll all be equally speedy.

A nonna will savour her coffee in the two or three sips required to empty the tiny cup and then it's time to go. No one orders a coffee and then stays for hours, no one gets out their laptop or scrolls through Instagram while their coffee cools (partly because it's not part of the culture in Italy and partly because coffee is served at perfect drinking temperature). A nonna might have a quick chat with the barista or an acquaintance but the purpose of coffee is to get the hit and get going. Knowing how Italian coffee culture works doesn't mean you need to obey those rules. If you want to sit and enjoy a coffee then you do exactly that. Italians know how to slow down and relax in general, they're just intense about coffee.

Never takeaway

Despite the fact that coffee is a fairly speedy affair, a nonna would never order a takeaway coffee. In fact, in Italy, except in train stations and airports, cafes rarely stock takeaway coffee cups, the concept is so foreign. Who doesn't have time to perch at the bar and drink the three sips of an espresso? Why wouldn't you make the time for that? Life should never be too busy to stop for coffee, and a nonna would never deny herself a coffee break. It's in these small moments, these pauses, that you can reflect, calm your mind and regroup before getting back to the hustle and bustle of life. So next time you're about to reach for your reusable cup to get a coffee to take back to your desk, put it down and go and take the time to have the coffee in a cafe. It won't take long but it will help you have a true break. Take a breath, drink an espresso. You'll be surprised the difference something so small can make to your life.

Dolci dolci dolci

Most coffee in Italy is served black, with a little sugar to cut through the bitterness. A nonna will tell you that milk is for a morning cappuccino or a baby's bottle, so if you're planning on having a cappuccino be sure to do so in the morning (or pretend that it's for a nearby child if it's later in the day). Milk is associated with breakfast in Italy so a milky coffee only makes sense to Italians in the morning.

Coffee consumed at the bar is often accompanied by a sweet pastry. Cannoli is a classic accompaniment, as is bombolone, an Italian-style donut filled with jam or custard. A simple biscotto is also commonly served with coffee and you might see Nonna dipping it into her espresso. Highly recommended!

Coffee first or last

Offering coffee immediately on your arrival when someone visits an Italian at home is thought to be quite rude. Doing so would suggest that your host does not want you to stay very long so they're rushing you out. That being said, Italians want to offer you things to eat and drink – it's in their DNA to feed you. So there's a weird tension between making you coffee and letting some time pass before offering you coffee.

Not all parts of Italian coffee culture make sense. The message here is drink coffee and serve it to your friends and family when they come over. Perhaps try not to overthink it as much as the Italians do!

TALES OF NONNA

'It's family folklore that Nonna would add a little bit of coffee to my bottle when I was a baby. People always panicked that I wouldn't sleep but I was apparently a good sleeper and Nonna swore that the coffee helped. I wish I knew if she really did put coffee in my bottle – it's a great story in any case, but something I would never recommend. The last thing a baby needs is caffeine! I still love coffee, of course, and I can drink an espresso and then go straight to sleep, so perhaps my nonna did build up my tolerance from a young age.' – J

Italian Coffee Guide

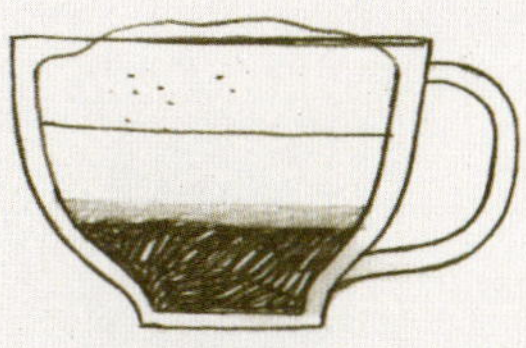

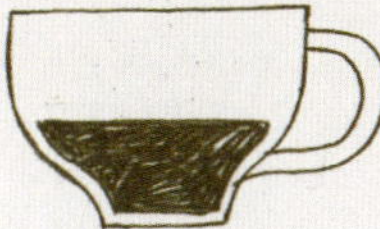

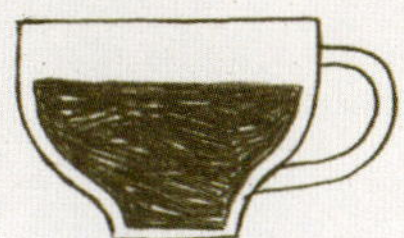

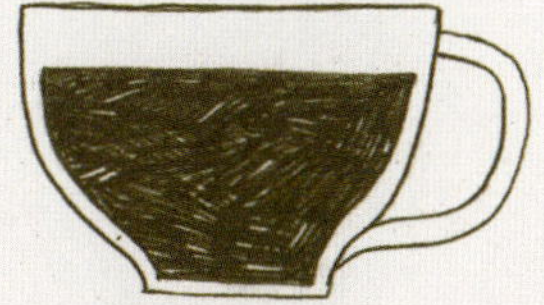

NONNA'S TIRAMISU

Tiramisu means 'pick, or pull, me up'. It is a delectable dessert that uses coffee, marscapone and biscuit fingers. Tiramisu lives up to its translation and can transform an ordinary meal into something very special.

Ingredients

180ml espresso coffee

2 tbsp coffee liqueur (Kahlua)

250ml mascarpone

250ml double cream

1 egg yolk

2 tbsp caster sugar

Seeds of ½ vanilla pod

12 Savoiardi biscuits (finger biscuits)

Cocoa powder for dusting

Serves four, or two hungry Italians

1. Combine the coffee and coffee liqueur in a bowl big enough to fit a Savoiardi biscuit.

2. In another bowl, add the mascarpone, double cream, egg yolk, sugar and vanilla seeds and whisk until smooth and creamy.

3. Dip each biscuit in the coffee mix, turning the biscuits over so that they're thoroughly coated.

4. Line the biscuits in a medium serving dish. You can line them in a single or a double layer.

5. Pour over the creamy mixture and spread evenly.

6. Dust the top with a thick layer of cocoa powder. You can serve immediately or refrigerate until needed.

Salute!

'Stop asking me if I want wine with my meal. I'm Italian, just pour.' – every Italian ever

Nonnas are partial to a glass of wine. They also enjoy a glass of prosecco ... and limoncello and grappa. You get the point – nonnas enjoy a drink. And why shouldn't they! They work hard and deserve to play just as hard.

But, as in many other aspects of their lives, nonnas take a no-nonsense approach to drinks. There's an Italian proverb, *Dire pane al pane e vino al vino,* that translates to 'Call bread, bread and wine, wine'. In English we might say 'Call a spade a spade' – but, let's be honest, bread and wine are much better than spades. Nonnas believe that wine should be accessible.

You won't find a nonna at a wine tasting, squishing and sniffing, and waxing lyrical about tannins. And you definitely won't find a nonna spitting wine into a spittoon. Wine is a simple pleasure for nonnas and they call it what it is.

Many nonnas make their own wine, often with their husbands and families, and this simple 'table wine' is consumed by adults at lunch and dinner. It's not so much about subtle flavours, but about the big bold flavours – a bit like the overall nonna approach to life.

So take a leaf out of nonna's book and uncomplicate your relationship with alcohol. You don't need a sommelier to help you choose the red to have with your pasta tonight. Grab a bottle of your favourite tipple and enjoy. Strengthen the link between food and wine and your relationship to alcohol will be a much healthier one, too. *Salute*!

Piazza

For many Italians, a meal without wine is like a day without sunshine. Food and wine are intertwined, even when it's just a casual drink with friends. Italians often like to consume their drink of choice in the *piazza* (the town square). It's the perfect people-watching opportunity. Many Italian bars also serve *spuntino* (finger food) with drinks. This allows you to enjoy the sweetness of doing nothing for a little longer. It also means you eat and drink and feel happy, which are all things nonnas love. In Italian culture, drinking is closely linked to food and mealtimes. Binge drinking is not the focus – the marriage of flavours between wine and food is. It's all part of appreciating the food served. Enjoy it with a glass of wine and good company.

Anni, amori e bicchieri di vino – non si contano mai

The passing years, lovers and bottles of wine should never be counted. Nonna is not one to keep tabs on such things and neither should you. Age is a number and many nonnas don't know their own birth date as they were born at home and such details were not recorded at the time of her birth. It's her approach to life that's important and we should all think less about our age and more about how we live. As for lovers and how many bottles of wine you drink, well, that's your business. Don't focus on numbers – just enjoy!

Aperitivo e digestivo

In addition to wine with a meal on special occasions, Italians enjoy a pre- and/or post-dinner drink. Given how much food Nonna has likely cooked it's a good idea to work up an appetite with an aperitivo. There are non-alcoholic aperitivo and digestivo options as this drink is linked to food, appetite and digestion rather than being about consuming alcohol. Once you've eaten all that food, a digestivo will help you do just as the name suggests: digest.

So every now and again go all out and plan your drinks for your meal. Nonnas are also quite keen to add some liquor to coffee, too. If you haven't experienced a spiked coffee before, you simply must – caffeine and alcohol are made to go together. A *caffè corretto* is an espresso 'corrected' with a pour of liquor, usually grappa, and is consumed later in the day, often after a meal. Italian alcohol culture is much healthier than in many other countries because it's so linked to food. Try to rethink your relationship with alcohol and see if you can view it as part of a meal rather than a stand-alone activity.

Spritz!

There are several styles of spritzes but the most popular are Aperol and Campari. They are both summer in a glass and many nonnas would happily down a spritz on a warm day. So find a decent bar, ideally one with people-watching possibilities, and enjoy a spritz in the sunshine. Nonna approved!

BELLINI

A Bellini is an incredibly special drink to behold. It can be made with fresh white peaches when the fruit is in season, but frozen puree or preserved white peaches will do just as well. The Bellini was invented by Giuseppe Cipriani, founder of the incredibly famous Harry's Bar in Venice. While Cipriani gets the credit for this drink, it should be said that marinating peaches in wine is a long-standing Italian tradition and one of the easiest desserts you can make. Drinking a Bellini at Harry's is a rite of passage for any tourist. For those of us who can't get there to experience it, here's how to make it at home.

Ingredients

100ml prosecco

50ml white peach puree

Serves one

1. Combine the prosecco and white peach puree in a chilled mixing glass. Stir until the two ingredients are combined.
2. Pour into a chilled champagne flute.
3. *Salute!*

There is no such thing as takeaway

Nonnas are from a pre-Uber Eats era; buying takeaway makes no sense when cooking is in their DNA. And nonnas are quick to point out that money spent on takeaway and eating out is money wasted.

'Just cook something easy,' any nonna would encourage. Italian food can be incredibly simple. And nonnas have many meals that they can throw together quickly and easily at any given time.

Take a leaf from Nonna's book and next time you reach for your phone to order takeaway, think of a quick meal you could cook. Ordering takeaway is a habit and one that can be broken. Have four or five go-to meals with ingredients you can have stocked in the pantry so you're never caught out with nothing to cook again.

Food in the pantry

Nonnas have a lot of food in their pantries and it means they can put food on the table with minimal effort if they need to. Having ready-made passata on hand at all times means dinner can be as simple as boiling water and cooking pasta. Stock your pantry with homemade preserves and pickles and you too will be able to prepare a delicious meal in next to no time – think olives, capers, dried tomatoes, preserved vegetables in oil or brine. For dessert, dried figs and peaches preserved in a sugar syrup always come in very handy.

Meals planned

Nonnas are organised, and they're willing to shop often. But if for some reason they know they cannot get to the store to buy food, they will get organised and plan their meals, buying everything they need in bulk. This means they never need to ask, 'What do you feel like for dinner?' (a foreign concept because dinner is not about what people feel like, it's about what Nonna is putting on the table).

Nonnas are also creatures of habit so they might eat similar foods on the same day each week. For example, many nonnas do not eat meat on Fridays for religious reasons so it's always a vegetarian meal or fish dish on a Friday at Nonna's house. Try this yourself. Make Wednesday risotto night. Make Monday pasta night. Make Friday pizza night. There are so many variations within each category that it won't get boring and getting a homemade meal on the table rather than from the delivery guy will be so much easier.

Better for you

The Mediterranean diet is held up as one of the healthiest ways to eat by nutritionists, doctors and even the World Health Organization. It is typically high in vegetables, fruits, whole grains, legumes, nuts, seeds and olive oil. All things that are particularly good for heart health. It also contains less meat and dairy than many other cuisines. Why you would consume large amounts of highly processed food or takeaway food over a Mediterranean diet makes no sense to nonnas.

Most takeaway foods have very high levels of salt and fat. When you cook at home you can control the ingredients that go into your meal, including the kinds of fat you use – remember, Nonna says to always cook with olive oil. These women are long-lived so they know a thing or two about what's good for you. Take your health into your own hands and cook fresh and delicious food yourself. Nonna wants you to be healthy and while she may encourage overeating, she only does so for high-quality delicious food, not takeaway.

Plastic waste

Nonnas are not the best environmentalists (they're certainly happy to wrap their couches in plastic) but when it comes to takeaway food containers, they're ecowarriors. Nonnas do not use straws, they do not buy takeaway, they generally go to delis and butchers and small grocers where less plastic waste is used than in the big supermarkets, and they do not buy takeaway coffee. Be like Nonna – go easy on the takeaway. Your health, your bank balance and the environment will thank you for it.

FIVE MEALS ANY ITALIAN CAN MAKE ANY TIME

The ingredients for these meals include pasta, arborio rice, olive oil, garlic, olives, anchovies, capers and saffron – all ingredients most nonnas have on hand all the time. Keep your pantry stocked with these key ingredients, add one or two fresh elements if you're feeling fancy, and you'll have an amazing dish ready in a flash.

1. Aglio e olio = spaghetti, olive oil, garlic, chilli, parsley (optional)
2. Pasta e broccoli = pasta, broccoli, olive oil, garlic, chilli
3. Puttanesca = pasta, olives, capers, anchovies, sugo, garlic
4. Pumpkin crostini soup = pumpkin, garlic, onion, old bread, tinned tomatoes
5. Risotto Milanese = rice, stock, saffron, onion

PASTA AGLIO E OLIO

Any nonna can whip up this meal at a moment's notice from ingredients she always has on hand. Be more Nonna and make sure you can, too. Mastering this recipe will mean you'll never go hungry.

Ingredients

80ml extra virgin olive oil

3 garlic cloves, crushed

½ tsp chilli flakes

Salt

Pepper

Parsley, finely chopped

400g spaghetti

Parmesan cheese

Serves four, or two hugnry Italians

1. In a small saucepan, gently heat the olive oil, garlic and chilli. Add a generous pinch of salt and some pepper.
2. Bring a large saucepan of salted water to a rolling boil. Add the spaghetti and cook for the recommended amount of time stated on the packet. Drain and return to saucepan.
3. Pour the hot oil mixture over the spaghetti. Add parsley and some more salt and pepper. Stir well.
4. Serve with freshly grated parmesan cheese.

Plant by the moon

Many nonnas are excellent gardeners, particularly when it comes to fruit and vegetables. In the same way they nurture their grandchildren, nonnas tend to and care for their tomato plants, grape vines and fruit trees. And unlike ungrateful grandchildren, the garden rewards them with an incredible bounty of delights.

Time in the garden is not just about growing food for the family to eat, it is also about escaping the pressures of everyday life and connecting with the earth. Gardening using the moon as a guide is important for many Italian gardeners. They believe that the moon can determine when water is distributed to plant roots, just as the moon controls the tides. With the moon as their gardening guide, nonnas know when a plant can be moved or harvested as well as how long a seed will take to germinate.

Regenerative gardening

Nonnas may not realise how ahead of the times they are with their regenerative approach to gardening. Nonnas add organic matter in the form of compost and manure to their veggie beds without a second thought. It's not permaculture to them, it's simply gardening. Improving the condition of the soil means a better crop so that's what they do. No need to buy chemicals that damage the soil. So take a leaf out of Nonna's gardening book and ditch the chemicals in favour of an organic approach. Your plants, your soil and your planet will thank you.

A seed saved

Nonnas are deeply practical so of course they save their own seeds. Why buy something when the plant will give it to you for free? Broad beans are one of the easiest seeds to save and many nonnas have a huge stash that they plant each year. Simply leave some pods on the most vigorous of your plants until they dry out completely. Pop the beans out of the pods (you'll know they are dry enough if you can push a fingernail into the bean and not leave a mark). Put the beans in a paper bag and plant them next year. Seeds saved from your veggie patch are best adapted to your conditions so your crops will just get better and better. Planting seeds you have saved yourself feels pretty good. Nonna would be so proud!

The moon

You might be surprised to learn that many nonnas plant and harvest according to the moon. This practice is an old one and as skeptical as you might feel about it, it's shocking how often nonnas are right about it. According to nonnas, most root vegetables, such as garlic, onions and potatoes, are best planted and harvested during a waning moon (*luna calante*). Carrots are an exception and they are best planted and harvested during a waxing moon (*luna cresente*). Crops like tomatoes, capsicum and eggplant are best planted and harvested during a waxing moon. The exception is only if you are not going to eat the produce fresh. If you plan on freezing or preserving your tomatoes, capsicum and eggplant, you should harvest on a waning moon. Broad beans and corn should be sown a few days before a full moon. There are no scientific studies to prove if nonnas are right about this but we trust them. They've been gardening successfully for so long and they learnt this stuff from their nonnas, that it's worth paying attention to.

Always in season

Nonnas wouldn't dream of growing or eating food out of season. For this reason they are master preservers. They take produce at the peak of the season when it's most abundant and cheapest to buy (if they haven't grown it themselves) and find ways to preserve it so they can enjoy it all year round. Some tomatoes become sugo, some are sun dried, and the last tomatoes of the season that won't ripen and remain green are pickled. Grapes are dried or pressed into wine. Peas and broad beans are shelled and frozen. Excess eggplant and zucchini are cooked and canned. Olives are cured or pressed into oil. Peaches are poached in a sugar syrup and preserved. Figs are dried. Meats are cured or smoked and hung to dry. You will never regret learning how to preserve produce. It's a skill that will serve you well for a lifetime.

Happiness is a full pantry

Nonnas stockpile food in their *cantinas* (pantry). They're not planning for the apocalypse, but they always want to be able to feed a large group of people should one suddenly appear. You'll find crates of apples and potatoes; rows of jars upon jars of sugo; barrels of homemade wine; flagons of pressed olive oil; prosciutto hanging from the ceiling; jars of jam and preserved fruits; and bundles of dried herbs, such as oregano and sage. Preserving the Italian nonna way will ensure you have a bounty of delicious things in a well-stocked larder throughout the entire year.

PRESERVING VEGETABLES

You could preserve a variety of vegetables using this method including artichokes, asparagus, beans, capsicum or zucchini.

Makes two, 350ml jars

Ingredients

500g of the vegetable you want to preserve

300ml white wine vinegar

2 garlic cloves, peeled

1 tsp peppercorns

Sprigs of rosemary or thyme

100ml lemon juice

450ml olive oil

1. Preparing the vegetable for preservation will depend on which vegetable you're using and the size of your jars. Trim beans and asparagus to fit in the jar. Slice zucchini. Remove the outer sections of artichokes until you're left with the heart. Slice capsicums and remove seeds.

2. Bring the vinegar and 200ml of water to the boil in a saucepan. Keep warm.

3. Heat a frypan or griddle pan on high heat. Char the vegetable you are preserving.

4. Drop the vegetables into the vinegar and leave for a few minutes.

5. Place a garlic clove, half the peppercorns and a sprig of rosemary or thyme into each jar.

6. Discard the vinegar, place half the chargrilled vegetables into each jar and cover with half of the lemon juice and olive oil. Add more olive oil if needed to completely cover the vegetables.

7. Keep jars in a cool dark place for six weeks before using. Once opened, keep the jar in the fridge.

CHAPTER TWO

~

LA FILOSOFIA DI NONNA

Dolce far niente

It's difficult to determine the origins of the phrase, perhaps because its inventors were too busy living it to record it. Dolce far niente *literally means 'the sweetness of doing nothing'. But the concept is both bigger and smaller than that.*

We rarely experience nothingness in our modern lives and the idea of enjoying the absence of anything is particular to Italians, who are quick to enjoy life rather than race through it. The secret to *dolce far niente* is to let it come naturally; you can't plan it. You simply relish in those moments when you find yourself doing nothing or drawn to doing nothing. Your mind is open. You notice the world around you. This is not mindfulness or meditation. It's a simple part of life and the everyday and is something you can easily incorporate into your daily life.

Find a balance

Nonnas can be incredibly busy women, but they all appreciate the essence of *dolce far niente*. They sit and watch passersby. They stand in the kitchen with an espresso and look out the window. They pause in the garden, putting down the rake or shovel. They sit with their friends after hours of gossiping and fall into a comfortable silence.

Nonnas have the patience to make fresh pasta, butcher their own meat, grow their own food, cure olives and juice blood oranges, but that doesn't mean their life is a constant chore. It's a balance between prioritising housework and enjoying the quietness of life. These things are actually connected for nonnas. They refuse to take the shortcuts modern life offers them and it makes the moments of idleness and reflection all the sweeter. Life is rooted in the earth, in growing things, in caring for people and animals, in making clothes and food. Choosing to spend time in these ways means they can appreciate the quiet, they can notice the changes in season, they can observe the world around them. Life becomes more meaningful because there's a balance between the chaos and the quiet, the mundane and the memorable, the busy and the still.

Reorganise inner energies

To be clear, it's not so much *doing* nothing as it is the absence of doing something. The Italian countryside is a particularly perfect backdrop for *dolce far niente*. The rolling hills, vineyards, olive groves and ancient buildings inspire a pause in activity. But your backyard, local park or lounge room can make a more than adequate substitute. There is no boredom here. There is no idleness. You remain very aware of the world around you. It's just a break from the action of your life. It's a moment where you can recharge and reorganise your inner energies (but Nonna would never use those words). Moments of nothing reduce stress levels. They help you see things in a different light. You get to put some space and distance between yourself and your life.

Slow down and smell the sugo

Dolce far niente is about truly enjoying and savouring a moment; relishing in its expansive emptiness. We don't always have to be doing things. The modern world makes us idealise busyness and productivity. Well, nonnas are here to tell us that we're prioritising the wrong things. Life can be lived slowly. We can suck the marrow from it (*osso bucco* anyone?). We can be languid. We can be thoughtful. We can enjoy nothing. And we'll be better for it.

The main time we seem to actually appreciate the sweetness of doing nothing is on weekends and holidays. They are the only times we *allow* ourselves to do nothing (and even then there's often an overwhelming amount of life admin and chores that get in the way of doing nothing). But you need to find ways to incorporate some space, some emptiness, some clarity into your daily life. You need to find ways to notice and appreciate the small things. You would never call a nonna lazy, even though they're sometimes idle. They appreciate the importance of these small moments where there is nothingness, and it's possibly because they are so busy that they can truly cherish the absence of anything. Their work ethic is strong but equally strong is their appreciation of not working, of taking life less seriously, of enjoying quiet contentment.

Nonnas know that we need to slow down and enjoy life. They're teaching us by example. So put your phone down, turn off the TV, take your earbuds out. Sit and be still. There is so much beauty in simplicity if you can only just find ways to relish the sweetness of absolutely nothing.

NOT DOING NOTHING

These things do not count *as doing nothing:*

Listening to music

Reading a book

Sunbathing

Chatting with friends

Watching TV

True *dolce far niente* is not just times when you're relaxed. It's the moments where you actively enjoy doing nothing, nothing at all. Find those moments. Notice them. Cherish them.

Sempre avanti

Simply translated sempre avanti mai indietro *means 'Always forward never backward'. It's a life philosophy for many Italians. No matter what terrible calamity has occurred, you will often hear a nonna sigh and say, 'Sempre avanti'. Their willingness to accept circumstances and just keep going is legendary.*

Nonnas are basically philosophers. They have a particular worldview shaped by their hard-earned life experiences and they won't be changing their minds any time soon. We have so much to learn from nonnas and their philosophical viewpoints. *Sempre avanti* is, in some ways, the nonna version of 'If life gives you lemons, make lemonade'. Nonnas are able to take so much in their stride and are some of the strongest and bravest people you will ever meet. So next time you're in a rut or feeling a bit down just think of Nonna and *sempre avanti mai indietro*.

The past is the past

Nonnas are not ones to dwell on the past. If you want to know about their lives as children you will need to ask them questions. (If you're lucky enough to have a living nonna, ask her questions! Ask her hundreds of questions.) Nonnas are very good at recognising that there is little point wallowing in the past – hope lies in the future. It might partly explain why they love their grandchildren so much. Given how obsessed we are with rehashing everything that has ever happened to us, there might be something in this for us to learn from. Looking back all the time can be exhausting and counterproductive. Although we perhaps shouldn't take it to nonna extremes, maybe you shouldn't hold on to every hurt or slight that has ever happened. Maybe you should try to ensure that your overall viewfinder is headed towards what comes next so you don't miss the exciting and wonderful things awaiting you.

Moving forward

Nonnas also believe that life is about continually moving forward in all things. Although they might not use these terms, nonnas believe in learning, growing and adapting. They are always trying to perfect what they do through repetition. Nonnas don't make pasta a few times and then decide they're done. They spend their lives perfecting the things they do. Nonnas don't fall victim to fads. They won't suddenly start creating fusion dishes. They see the beauty in doing things well and doing them often. So pick a thing and get really good at it. The way to get good at it is to do it a lot. A. Lot. Keep doing it. Teach other people how to do it. Enjoy doing it and doing it well. Keep doing it for as long as you possibly can.

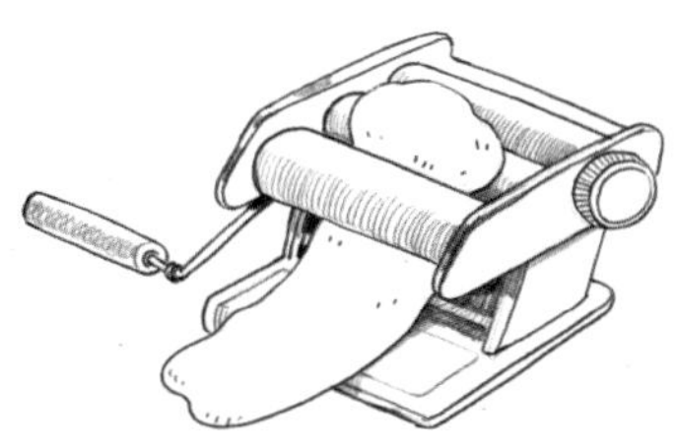

Eyes on the horizon

With eyes on the horizon, those who follow *sempre avanti* as a life philosophy recognise that life is linear and ever-changing. There is real comfort in that. Change may be the only constant in life and always moving forward allows you to embrace that change and keep going. Life marches on and we need to march with it, nonna style (so pretty slowly, actually). Keep your eyes on the horizon. Look out for the exciting things coming your way.

Piano piano

You will rarely see a nonna frantically rushing. 'Slowly, slowly' is a nonna's life philosophy. It's her version of 'slow and steady wins the race'. But for a nonna there is no race. She might bustle about but she's not madly rushing from thing to thing. Life is to be enjoyed! So, take a deep breath and take it one step at a time.

If you're to appreciate moments of nothingness and have a *dolce far niente* approach to life, then it's best to go *piano piano*. Nonnas are languid but efficient in their movements. They are disinclined to rushing or flitting from thing to thing. They do not race, they do not run, they do not double-book themselves. Nonnas are far less stressed than the rest of us and yet their first principles are to cook with raw ingredients, to clean until their homes sparkle and to grow their own produce.

What is their secret? *Piano piano*! Nonnas value time. They know that every moment is precious and you need to savour each day, so it's best to avoid multi-tasking and overcommitting. Their unrushed approach allows them to enjoy their time. So next time you think you should squeeze a few more things into your day, take a step back. Just because you can doesn't mean you should. By doing less you might just find yourself enjoying more.

Slow down

Nonnas do not accept the pace of the modern world. They encourage us to slow down and enjoy what we're doing. Preparing dinner is not a chore to rush through. We shouldn't be checking the time when having coffee with a friend. Nonnas slow life down so they can enjoy it. They don't glorify being busy. They don't think rushing makes someone seem important. It's so easy for us to do too much at once: we have smart phones that let us call a friend while ordering food and checking when the next bus will arrive. We're pressured to be productive every single second of our lives and therefore skim through days in such a superficial, rushed way. The nonna way of life offers us an escape from this completely unnecessary hyper-productivity. Value what is truly important in life. Nonnas know that the best pace of life is slow. *Piano piano*!

One thing at a time

Nonnas do one thing at a time. They do it well and they do it thoroughly. Nonnas leave themselves plenty of time to complete each task allowing themselves moments of *dolce far niente* in between. Nonnas can make a three-course meal for twelve people without breaking a sweat. And that's partially because they go slowly slowly. *Piano piano!*

Watch the world go by

Nonnas enjoy sitting on their front porch watching the world go by. Knowing the comings and goings of one's neighbours is almost a national Italian sport invented by nonnas. Nonnas probably make incredible police witnesses because they notice and remember everything. That said, sitting outside and quietly observing the movements of neighbours, the chirping of birds and the buzzing of bees is a great way to slow life down. We should all do it more. *Piano piano*!

La dolce vita

La dolce vita *is a well-known Italian phrase but the secret of how to embrace* la dolce vita *is less well-known. The phrase literally translates as 'the sweet life' but it's really about the good life. It's not so much Marcello Mastroianni pursuing beautiful women across Rome in a film as it is making a life that is full of the important things – family, friends, adventures, love, good food, wine.*

The good life can mean different things to different people, but it's quite simple for nonnas: it is about small moments of joy. The joy of holding a new grandchild, the joy of seeing those you love enjoying the food you have made, the joy of watching the trees and plants you tend offer fruit and vegetables, the joy of seeing and catching up with friends. Learn to notice and appreciate these small moments of joy and you will discover *la dolce vita*. The good life will bring you happiness, it will make you calm and appreciative, it will allow you to revel in the wonders of life. If the modern condition is anxiety, *la dolce vita* is the cure.

Slow down

The *piano piano* approach mentioned earlier and the idea of *dolce far niente* are both essential elements of *la dolce vita*. Slow down and savour each spare moment. When travelling, do not rush from sight to sight or pack your schedule full of activities; stop to enjoy a leisurely meal in a beautiful setting, wander without a destination in mind, put your phone away and just soak up the atmosphere. When working, try not to get caught up in the glorification of busy. Take a long lunch and eat good food. Don't eat at your desk or look at your phone. Block out weekends and make NO PLANS. See what you feel like doing on any given day and do that. Nonnas are busy women but no matter how many chores or tasks they have to do, they still make the time to enjoy the sweetness of a spare moment in each day. Living life this way is achievable for anyone who sets their mind to it.

Get your hands dirty

Nonnas get their hands dirty in all kinds of ways: in elastic pasta dough, in the fresh earth while gardening, in the sticky skins of grapes as they make wine, or in silky olive oil when tossing a salad. Nonnas want to enjoy every sensation this life has to offer them. They want to connect fully and deeply on a visceral level with the things they do, from chores to work to fun. They want to devour every experience in as many ways as possible. Nonnas like to get their hands dirty metaphorically, too – they get involved, they step in, they help others. They do not hang back if help is needed. They do not observe when they can participate. Never hesitate to get your hands dirty, literally or metaphorically. You'll be a happier person for it.

A life of pleasure

The encapsulation of *la dolce vita* is a life of pleasure. Pleasure doesn't have to come from indulgence. It can come from prioritising moments of stillness over moments of noise, time with family over time on Facebook, time in nature over time with the TV blaring. You really only need to look to nonnas to see what's important and what matters.

... All of that said, one should definitely frolic in the Trevi Fountain should the opportunity ever present itself. Nonna would definitely encourage it and Anita Ekberg certainly made it look like fun in the film *La Dolce Vita*.

The nonna way

When it comes down to it, the nonna approach to *la dolce vita* isn't so much about *what* you do as it is *how* you do it. Nonnas have a zest for life. They are highly expressive and passionate people but they don't take things too seriously (except for card games and faith, more on that later). Really, nonnas just want to have fun. So, add some zest to your life and try to fill it more with metaphorical splashes in the Trevi Fountain.

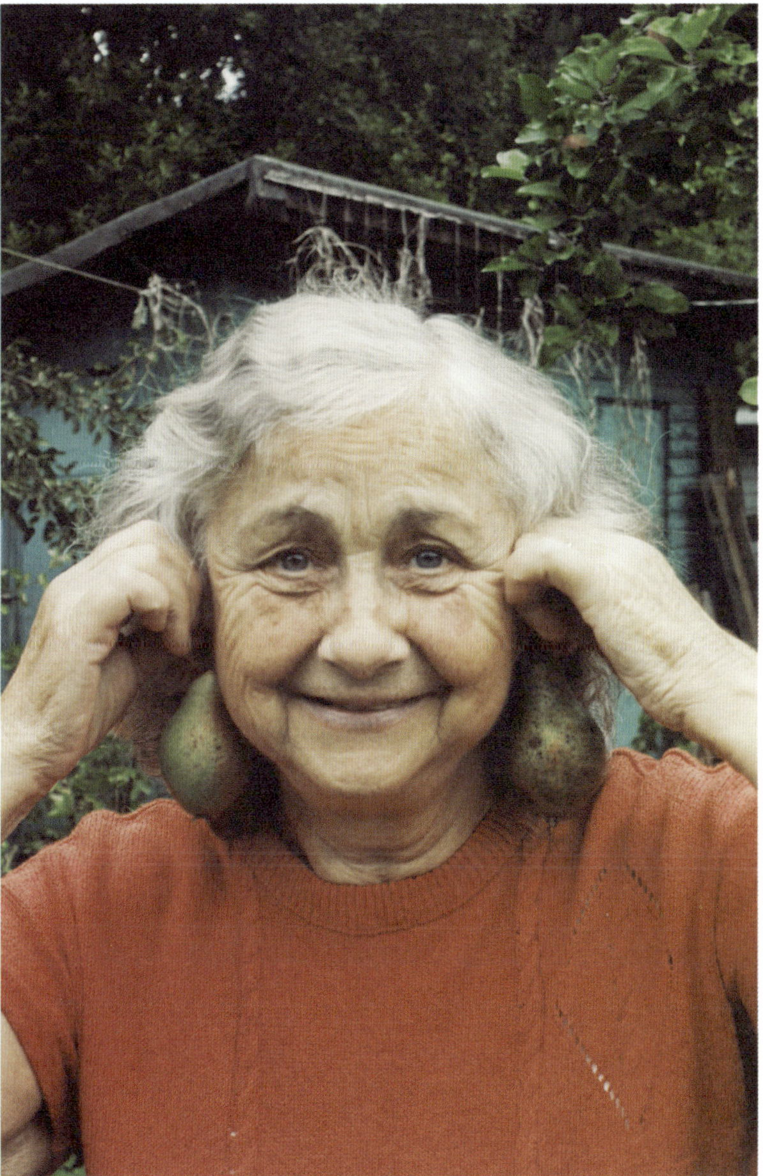

LA DOLCE VITA

Of course, frolicking in the Trevi Fountain these days could result in imprisonment, so here are some alternatives that will help you free your inhibitions and embrace joy and levity.

~

Dance in the rain

~

Sing in the shower

~

Kiss your partner at the movies

~

Float on your back in the ocean or in a pool and look up at the sun

~

Order dessert for dinner

~

Dance in the supermarket aisles

~

Dress up at an op shop

~

Turn up the volume and sing loudly in the car

~

Roll down a hill or ride down a hill on your bike

~

Have a picnic in your living room

~

Put on your favourite clothes and take yourself out on a 'self-date'

~

Howl at the moon

BRUTTI MA BUONI (UGLY BUT GOOD)

These crunchy on the outside, chewy on the inside almond biscuits originated in central Italy. They may not look particularly good but they are definitely delicious. Only a nonna would give a biscuit a name like this with her irreverent humour and direct style.

Ingredients

5 egg whites

500g caster sugar

1kg ground almonds (skin on)

1¼ tbsp cocoa

Pinch of salt

Makes a lot but don't worry, they never last long

1. Beat the egg whites, gradually adding the caster sugar, until stiff and glossy.

2. Fold in the ground almonds, cocoa and salt until combined.

3. Place tablespoon-sized balls of the mixture on a lined baking tray.

4. Bake at 180°C for 20 to 30 minutes. The biscuits should sound hollow when tapped on the bottom.

5. Leave to cool and then store in an airtight container.

Se Dio vuole

While nonnas advocate a carefree approach to life, religion and religious practices are very important to them. Their spirituality is linked to religious faith and the teachings of the church provide them with a firm foundation for life.

Most Italians, particularly older Italians, belong to the Roman-Catholic faith. Today, approximately 80 per cent of the Italian population is Christian, and 75 per cent is Roman-Catholic. Many nonnas attend mass on Sundays, visit the cemetery to tend to loved ones' graves and will generally pray daily, alone or in a group, using the aid of rosary beads.

Older Italians may have icons in their homes such as pictures of saints, the holy family and statuettes of the Madonna and Jesus. Religion itself may not be for everyone, but having an insight into how it influences the nonna approach to life will help you to understand what makes a nonna tick and how her faith helps her through life. As the western world becomes more secular, we won't have as many people of strong faith to look to for spiritual guidance.

Strength in faith

Nonnas approach religion in the same way they approach every aspect of life: with boundless energy and enthusiasm. The Pope is basically a rock star to them. The local priest is often a close friend and regular dinner guest. Nonnas take tremendous strength from their faith and although we may not be able to embrace it as fully as they do, we can look to what it offers them and see how it might be useful for us. For example, the phrase *se Dio vuole,* meaning 'God willing', provides comfort to nonnas in times of sadness as well as happiness. Many nonnas believe that what happens in life is determined by God and therefore they worry less because they have faith in God – it's kind of like an Italian version of que será será. Nonnas also take great comfort in realising their own insignificance in God's larger plan. They do not prize themselves as individuals so much as they see themselves as part of a larger family and community group with church being a large part of that. The perspective this view offers is undeniable and can help you realise your insignificance in the grand scheme of life. We can become so self-obsessed that we forget that we are just specks of dust in the larger cosmos. What we do matters because we matter, but not as much as we think it does.

Do unto others

Nonnas take from religion a belief system to live by. They treat others as they wish to be treated (card games are exempt of course). They love their neighbours (though to be fair most nonnas' neighbours are their own family). They strive to be kind to all. If you wanted a guide to being a kind and good person that would pretty much sum it up, right? Look to nonnas' attempts to be kind and good and apply it to your own life. 'Do unto others' is an easy moral check to make sure you're heading in the right direction. Come back to it whenever you are unsure how to behave or proceed. What would Nonna do?

Patron saints

Many older Italians will observe holy days on the Italian religious calendar. Most nonnas have a patron saint, usually one from their region, who they pray to regularly. They might also have statues, or religious medallions with this saint. There are saints to pray to when you lose something, when you drive a car, for better eyesight and even for winemaking. These specific saints are believed to help in these specific situations. Here are the five most popular saints in Italy who you can call on in times of need:

1. St Anthony – the saint to pray to when you lose something

2. St Jude – the saint to pray to for hopeless or desperate causes

3. St Catherine of Siena – the saint to pray to if there is a fire

4. St Francis of Assisi – the saint to pray to if you have a sick animal

5. Padre Pio – the saint to pray to if you need healing

Cleanliness is next to godliness

Many nonnas are intense cleaners. The surfaces of their homes sparkle and the forty-year-old stove looks exactly as it did on the day it was installed. The smell of *varechina* (bleach) is often in the air at Nonna's house. For these nonnas, cleanliness is next to godliness. There is something to be said for keeping a baseline of cleanliness in your home. That baseline doesn't need to be as high as Nonna's – nobody can clean like that woman – but a decent level of cleanliness makes life just that little bit more manageable, especially when life throws you a curveball.

Church as community

Religious nonnas derive a great deal of support from their church. Religion is important as it provides a sense of community and culture. As well as a time for reflection, church can be a social occasion and a time to see friends and family. You need to follow Nonna's lead on this and make sure you make/find time to reflect on the bigger things and spend time with those you love.

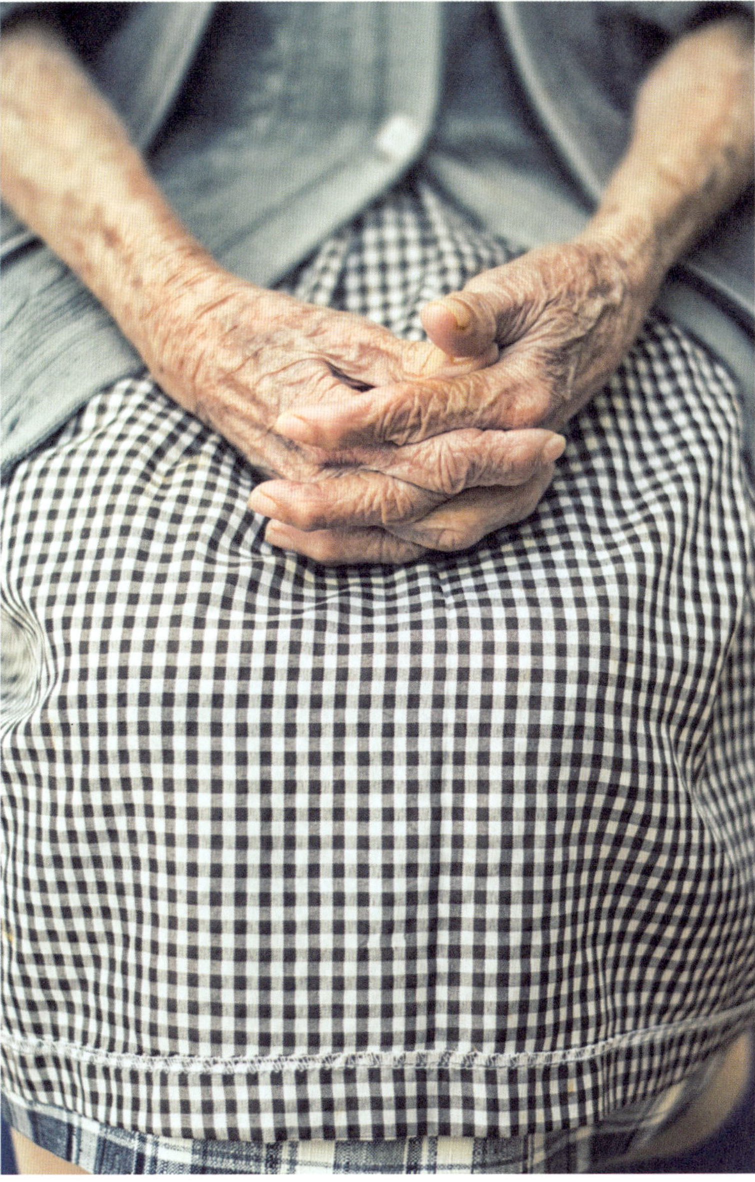

CANNOLI DI CARNEVALE

Carenevale is a religious festival celebrated before Lent. Cannoli are widely consumed during this period as Lent is a time of fasting. A cannolo is a fried, tube-shaped pastry filled with a ricotta-based filling. The ricotta is usually blended with vanilla, chocolate, lemon or pistachio.

Ingredients

80g unsalted butter, cubed

375g plain flour

1 egg

2 egg yolks

½ cup Marsala

Vegetable oil for deep frying

80g shelled pistachios, finely chopped

Icing sugar for dusting

Filling

300g ricotta

200g mascarpone

100g caster sugar

Zest of 1 lemon

Makes 20 cannoli

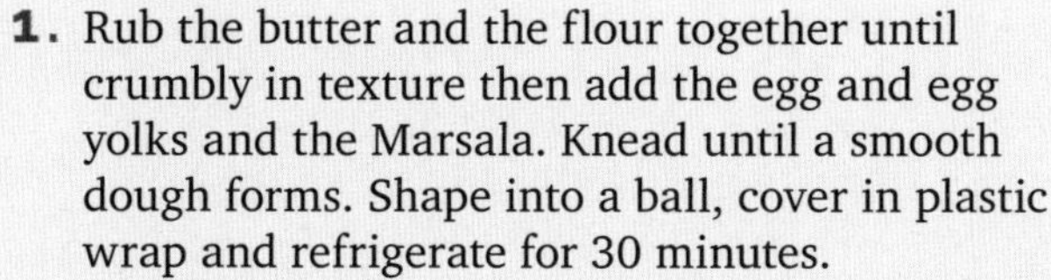

1. Rub the butter and the flour together until crumbly in texture then add the egg and egg yolks and the Marsala. Knead until a smooth dough forms. Shape into a ball, cover in plastic wrap and refrigerate for 30 minutes.

2. To make the filling, place the ricotta, mascarpone, caster sugar and lemon zest in a food processor and blend until smooth.

3. Roll the dough on a floured surface until 1–2mm thick. Using a round cutter, cut 20 rounds from the dough. Wrap each circle around a cannoli mould (or a piece of dowel if you don't have a cannoli mould), wetting and pressing the point of overlap.

4. Fry the cannoli on their moulds in very hot vegetable oil for 4 minutes. Remove from the oil and remove the moulds. Fry the cannoli again for 5 minutes to cook the inside. Leave to cool completely.

5. Place the filling into a piping bag with a plain nozzle and fill the cannoli shells from each end. Sprinkle both ends with the pistachios and dust with icing sugar.

Celebrate what you have

You will not find Nonna mindlessly scrolling through Instagram as she covets the lives of those whooshing past.

She might be competitive about her gnocchi, but Nonna is happy to see those around her do well. You also won't find Nonna worrying about the little things. She can see the big picture and has lived long enough to know that the small stuff doesn't matter! Push the small stuff aside and celebrate what you have.

Be mindful

One of the most mindful exercises you can do is to make and handroll pasta or gnocchi. Your worries will fall away as you knead and roll. Making pasta and gnocchi is actually surprisingly easy – it just takes a bit of time, something you think you don't have (you do). Nonnas know that there is always time to make fresh pasta. And while they roll it out, their minds lighten and their troubles dissipate. Forget yoga or colouring-in – making pasta is true mindfulness.

Happy with simple

Nonnas' tastes run simple. They use the same pots and pans their entire lives, they keep their clothes in good condition and wear them repeatedly, they cook from first principles. Nonnas don't pay attention to fads or fashion. They have their style in food, fashion and life and they stick with it. They want life to be simple so they can enjoy it. It's the enjoying of it that's the important part. Think about how you can simplify your life and start doing it. Do you really need subscriptions to multiple streaming sites? Do you really need a new smart phone? What might your life look like without these things?

Less meat

Nonnas do not make spaghetti Bolognese. It's not a thing. If they do make a meat ragu they would serve it with fettucine or tagliatelle or a small-shaped pasta – bolognese sauce slips right off spaghetti as any nonna will tell you. But the truth of it is that many nonnas save meat for special occasions only. The cost of meat has been prohibitive, plus nonnas know their way around cooking vegetables! Reducing your meat intake is likely to have health-positive outcomes and will definitely have environmental benefits. So cut back on the meat and embrace the nonna diet of carbs, legumes and vegetables.

Ditch the phone

Nonna would like to see you set some boundaries with your phone. She has no idea what you're up to on it, but she recommends:

- setting a time limit or curfew on apps
- turning off push mail
- never using your phone in bed
- charging your phone in a remote part of your house or apartment.

Think of how many more hours Nonna has had available in her life because she didn't have a mobile phone. You have no excuse! Put the phone down and pick up the pasta machine. Your mind and body will thank you for it.

ZA
410 WA

TOP WAYS TO CELEBRATE WHAT YOU HAVE

If Nonna was to name her top ways of celebrating the life you have she might say:

1. Take a deep breath, notice and enjoy being alive.
2. Show your love – drop an old friend a line or send a postcard to someone you've been meaning to get in touch with.
3. Take a break from social media – if you're a true addict, it doesn't have to be a whole day. Try it for an afternoon. Leave your phone at home and go for a long walk or head to the beach.
4. Cook a delicious and generous meal and then watch those you love enjoying it.
5. Polish shoes, mend clothes, repair what is broken.
6. Relish in the success of others.

NONNA'S GNOCCHI

These soft pillows of deliciousness are a staple in any nonna's cooking arsenal. The ratio of flour to potato is crucial – they must be firm enough to hold together but not hard. Rolling gnocchi should be a meditative experience – let the process allow you to clear your mind and enjoy the simplicity of a repetitive, mindful task.

Ingredients

1kg Desiree potatoes

2 eggs

Pinch of nutmeg, freshly grated

Pinch of salt

200g plain flour, plus extra for dusting

Serves four, or two hungry Italians

1. Place the potatoes in a large pot and cover with cold water. Bring to the boil then reduce the heat to simmer and cook for 30 minutes. Drain, then peel the skins.

2. Pass the potatoes through a potato ricer onto a lightly floured workbench. (A potato ricer is called a *schiacciapatate* in Italian. This utensil is non-negotiable – if you don't have one, buy one. At a pinch you could use a *passa tutto*.)

3. Make a well in the centre of the potatoes and place the eggs, nutmeg, salt and flour into it. Knead until you form a firm dough, adding more flour if the dough is too soft.

4. Roll the dough into 2.5cm strips. Cut each strip into 2.5cm pieces. Roll each piece on a corrugated gnocchi board if you have one or use the tines of a fork to form indentations (this allows the gnocchi to catch more sauce). Sprinkle with some flour and cover with a tea towel to prevent them from drying out.

5. Boil the gnocchi in well-salted water until they rise to the top. You may need to do this in batches so as not to overcrowd the saucepan.

6. Serve with your favourite pasta sauce.

CHAPTER THREE

~

AMORE E FAMIGLIA

Love like a nonna

In Italian culture, family is highly valued and forms part of the social and community fabric. A nonna loves her family, her friends, her community, her church and she goes to great lengths to foster and strengthen these relationships. Because love is everything. Nonnas don't hold back when it comes to love. They love deeply, passionately and excessively.

A nonna would never withhold her love. She wouldn't tone it down for any reason. Nobody loves with as much reckless abandon as a nonna. She also loves unconditionally. If you're in her family she loves you. It's that simple. We should all try to open our hearts to love like a nonna.

Let's get physical

A high level of physical contact is considered natural and normal among Italians. Italian men and women greet acquaintances and friends with a kiss on both cheeks. Love is physical as well as emotional for nonnas. Nonnas are likely to grab those cheeks and give them a good squeeze especially if a chubby baby is brought anywhere near their vicinity. She might not talk about how much she loves you but she'll hug you until you can barely draw breath. She'll always make your favourite foods when you visit. She'll take you to places she knows you want to go. She'll care for, and about, you in truly deep and meaningful ways. She will do all this without expecting much at all in return. She'll want you to visit often, eat and enjoy her food of course, but those are pretty much all the strings that are attached to a nonna's love. And those strings are pretty delicious. Think about the people you love and the ways you can show them that you love them that will be meaningful to them. That's how you love like a nonna.

Show love

Nonnas are highly expressive of joy and love. Their eyes have a special twinkle and they are always ready with a hug and a big smile. Nobody will love you the way a nonna loves you. We can all work at offering the same big love to others. Show love at every opportunity. Never miss a chance to tell or show someone you love them. Show your love physically to your family and friends and incorporate hugs, touches and caresses into your life whenever appropriate to do so.

Sprinkle love

To a nonna everyone is *cara* or *gioia* (dear or darling). She simply sprinkles love wherever she goes. Her big heart is open and she is never afraid of it being broken. She is willing to love big and boldly. Go on, love like a nonna!

TALES OF NONNA

'When I got married I wanted to include my nonna and nonno in the ceremony. I heard about a ritual where someone who has been married for a long time holds the wedding rings and warms them at the start of the service.'

'I asked my nonni if they would do this and despite not really understanding why I wanted them to hold the rings they agreed. It turned out to be a special moment and felt like a blessing from them. Nonna told me she put extra love into my ring.' – J

52

54

Play to win

Nonnas can be incredibly sweet and loving. But, as previously mentioned, they have a ruthless streak and when they play cards or tombola (bingo), they play to win.

The most popular card games in Italy include *briscola*, *scopa*, *tresette* and *bestia*. These games are played using Italian cards and these can be purchased at many Italian delis. Playing games is an important part of the social fabric of a nonna's life. Some Italian card games can be played alone but most require other people. It's a great way to spend time with friends without spending a huge amount of money. During these card games, which at first seem like a nonchalant affair, emotions can quickly flare up for even the most passive of Italian pensioners. So take a leaf out of Nonna's book: bring your friends together, serve them coffee and biscotti, chat and laugh … then destroy them at cards.

Earning your wins

Some people believe that allowing children to win helps to build their confidence and self-esteem. Nonnas did not get this memo. A nonna would *never, ever* let you win. It doesn't matter how old you are, how bad a day you've had, how hard you're trying, nonnas play to win every single time. Nonnas want the best for us but that doesn't mean they want us to think that the universe will deliver it to us unearned. If you win, you deserved to win – plain and simple.

Tough love

Nonnas believe in tough love. They don't think letting you win is doing you any favours, so they don't do it. Whether it's *briscola, tresette, scopa* or the perfectly named *bestia*, nonnas bring their A game and they expect you to as well. They know that in the real world nobody is going to let you win and you have to earn what you get. A bit of tough love is good for us. It keeps us grounded and shows how the world really works. Don't get jaded, get even.

Work hard, play hard

Nonnas work hard and they play hard. They value both aspects of life and couldn't do one without the other. Passion is part of everything they do. Why play if you're not going to be passionate about the outcome? Why cook if you're not going to do it with care and love? Why love if you're not going to be all-consumed by it? The nonna approach to life advocates passion in all things. We could all do with more passion in our lives. Be bold, play to win, but also just play. Make games and fun a regular part of your daily life.

TALES OF NONNA

'After my Nonna had a stroke in her eighties she could no longer walk, her speech was impaired and she couldn't cook. But she could play cards. When she played, she was still exactly the same person she had been pre-stroke. I don't remember winning a single game of briscola against her but I must have. I do, however, remember her throwing down the ace of suns (highest card) to take my three of suns (second-highest card) with a triumphant, 'Toh!' and a glint of world domination in her eye. Not even a stroke could take that spirit from her.' – J

Family is everything

A nonna's priority is always her family. With nonnas at the centre, the essence of the Italian spirit is welcoming and passionate.

Find occasions to bring your family together and love them like Nonna would – unequivocally, completely, reverently. Take a moment to reflect on your own priorities. Are they clear to you? Are you happy with them? Is there anything you need to reassess?

Famiglia

Nonnas will do literally anything for their families. They are usually eager to welcome new additions to the family through birth, adoption or marriage. Grandchildren are precious and showering them with love is something nonnas excel at. Parents of young children often report that Italy is a great country to travel to with young children because the locals are so accommodating. That comes down to nonnas. In a nonna's eyes children are the greatest blessing. Sure, they love their grandchildren, but they're happy to love any child that's at hand.

Custodians of culture

Nonnas are keepers of their culture. They are happy to pass on what they know to the next generation, if asked. This is how recipes and memories will be kept alive. These women need to be celebrated for the role they play in their families and their culture. As we all move to faster-paced ways of life, nonnas can remind us how things were done back in the day. They can teach us traditional ways of doing things, from gardening to cooking to cheating at cards. Again, if you have access to a nonna, your own or someone else's, ask them questions and write down their recipes. Having the life skills of a nonna will always be useful – they are the custodians of culture and they are willing to pass on what they know.

Senza complimenti

Senza complimenti means 'don't be shy, help yourself, don't hold back', and you'll often hear it from a nonna. Whether or not you're family, she wants you to feel at home and comfortable. This extends to serving yourself food and wine and shows you're part of the family. So take note of Nonna's generous and hospitable spirit and adopt a *senza complimenti* approach.

The heart of the family

There is no doubt that nonnas form the heart of a family. They are the ones gathering the family for any occasion they can think of – birthdays, important religious days, Sundays. They're the ones constanly cooking to ensure a mountain of food is served. Nonnas are irreplaceable but their role can be passed on once they're no longer with us. Gather your family around you; hold them tight. If you don't have a family or aren't close to the one you do have, you can always make your friends your family.

Nonnas to the front

We need to celebrate nonnas and their unique role in their communities and families. These women are the fabric that holds their families together and should be revered. So next time you see a nonna out and about take a moment to chat to her. Ask about her grandchildren. Ask about her tomato crop. Ask about her lasagna recipe (béchamel or no béchamel, that is the question!). Ask her the best time to plant parsley seeds. Nonnas to the front!

TALES OF NONNA

'I was so happy when my daughter was born and introducing her to my nonna, her bisnonna *(great grandmother), was so special. My nonna didn't appreciate that I thought it was a bad idea for her to squeeze my five-hour-old daughter's cheeks.'*

'Every time I looked over she was squeezing her cheeks, and I mean really squeezing. I asked my mum to get Nonna to cool it but she had no luck either. I pretended I needed to feed my daughter and held her closely. She started to scream like mad. I could not soothe her. Nonna asked for her back and I reluctantly agreed. Nonna immediately went back to her cheek-squeezing ways and my daughter quieted right down. To this day, my daughter loves it when we squeeze her cheeks, just like Nonna used to.' – S

Better together

Nonnas know that almost any job is better shared. That's why they are always willing to help out family, friends and neighbours with time-consuming jobs – they know it will be more pleasant together and that the favour will be returned.

Often Italian family members all come together for large-scale food and wine production, sharing the spoils. It's a fantastic approach to life: do it together, share what you do.

A job shared

Nonnas understand the fun and joy of performing a task as a group. Sitting alone and shelling peas can be incredibly boring and tedious but add some siblings, music, friends and grandchildren and suddenly you have a party. The job gets done, the produce gets shared and everyone has a smile on their face. So make a day of it with friends and family whether it's preserving, cooking, gardening or any other task. It's always better doing it together.

Community

Sharing jobs and doing tasks together is also a simple way to build communities. If you start a street passata day it's pretty much guaranteed that people will come and new communities and friendship groups will form. The joy of making something, anything, together can spark real connections.

NONNA'S FAVOURITE DAYS

Tomato day

Tomato day is probably the biggest production event in any Italian household. And it's a group activity. Family members and friends start early, washing the tomatoes that are to be transformed into passata and bottled for the year ahead. The tomatoes are scored and then boiled and peeled. The skinless tomatoes are then put through a *passa tutto* (these can be electric or manual and they puree the tomato flesh and separate the seeds) and what comes out is liquid gold. The sauce is then bottled, and the bottles are boiled to seal and preserve them. This is a whole-day affair and can involve hundreds of kilos of tomatoes. Having a large group of people makes light work and the social aspect is an important part of the day (as is the lunch). Everyone leaves with enough bottles to see them through until next year. It's magical! And you can do it, too. Invite people over, buy some boxes of tomatoes, gather old jars or bottles, buy or borrow a *passa tutto* and perform each step together as a group. You'll be amazed by how much you can achieve in a day with a willing group of people.

Vino day

Vino day is another big one on the Italian calendar. Turning grapes into wine is an involved process that requires some specialist skill, knowledge and equipment. But many nonni make delicious table wine year after year. If you're able to get yourself invited to a vino day be sure to go and take notes! The skills and knowledge about how to make wine at home are being lost and that is a tragedy.

Salami day

Some Italians have not-so-fond memories of salami day, the day when a complete pig would arrive in the morning and relatives and friends would spend the day turning it into sausages, cured meat such as salami and prosciutto, doing unspeakable things with the offal and just generally stinking up the place. All that said, making your own sausages is incredibly satisfying and much healthier and more delicious than the sausages you buy. Salami festivals are becoming popular where knowledge is shared about how to make salami, so sign up if you're keen to learn. It's an incredible life skill to have.

NONNA'S PASSATA

We're going to start simple here and just make six litres of passata. Any nonna would always make a much larger batch so feel free to multiply the recipe. Be mindful not to multiply the salt though and go by taste.

Makes six, one-litre bottles

Ingredients

8kg roma tomatoes

Iced water

70g salt

6 large basil leaves
(This is somewhat controversial. Some nonnas always add a basil leaf to each jar of passata and some don't. I had one nonna who did – Vincenzina – and one who didn't – Paolina – so I put a basil leaf in every second bottle to try to make everyone happy. Go with your gut.)

1. Score each tomato skin with a cross pattern on the base. Blanch them in boiling water for 1 minute. Remove and refresh them in iced water. Peel off the skins.

2. Pass the tomatoes through a *passa tutto* to extract the juice. Pass the pulp through a few times to get all the goodness possible. Compost any remaining pulp (add some garden lime to help the compost with the acidity of the tomato pulp).

3. Mix the salt through the passata.

4. Place a basil leaf (or not) into each of 6 sterilised 1-litre bottles. Pour in the passata, leaving a gap at the top of each bottle. Seal tightly with a capping machine.

5. Stand the six bottles in a large saucepan and weave tea towels around them to prevent them from breaking. Cover with cold water. Bring to a boil and then reduce to a simmer and boil for 30 minutes.

6. Leave the bottles to cool in the saucepan overnight.

7. Store in a dark, cool spot. Properly sealed bottles of passata can last for a couple of years. Use whenever a jar of passata is required. Nonna will be so proud!

A nonna needs a nonno

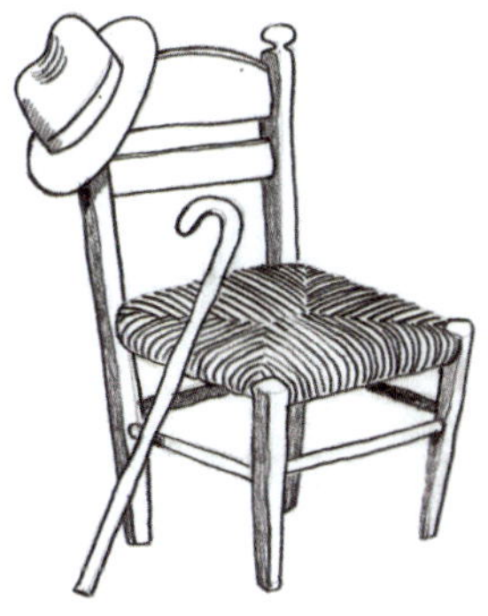

Okay, so 'needs' might be pushing it, but a nonna and a nonno are a formidable duo. They have a unique bond and although they may disagree a lot and loudly, they know each other incredibly well and do so many things together.

The thing about a nonna and a nonno is that they have been doing the same things together for a very long time. They have gardened together, preserved together, danced together, raised children together, made wine together – all of the things that make an Italian household. As we lead more separate lives than ever, we need to remember the joy of shared tasks.

The same cloth

Nonnas and nonnos are often cut from the same cloth and have very similar beliefs, for example about religion and family. Nonna and Nonno agree that you should visit more, for example. They're unanimous about that. Their shared beliefs mean that they're well suited at doing stuff together and sharing a life.

Find yourself a nonno

Nonnos are rarely perfect, but they are usually perfect for their nonna. Italian women today are marrying much older than previous generations. Today, the average age of a woman on her wedding day in Italy is thirty-one whereas in the 1970s it was twenty-five. Italians of the current 'nonna and nonno generation' married even younger. So, they grew up together in many ways and have an intimate knowledge of one another. Find yourself someone you can change and grow with over the years. Find yourself someone who will press the grapes, process the tomatoes and pick the beans with you. Doing things together and having shared interests is so important in a relationship and it's something nonni take completely for granted.

Together forever

Until 1970, it was illegal for a couple to divorce in Italy. There was simply no legal way to divorce. Divorce in Italy became easier starting in 2016. Before then, an Italian couple that wished to divorce had to separate for at least three years. The period of separation before divorce proceedings can commence is now much shorter. All that said, even if they legally could, most nonni would never divorce regardless of the state of their marriage. In traditional Italian culture, marriage is for life. Nonni also seem particularly good at finding ways to live together in their own kind of harmony. Perhaps if we focused more on spending time with those we love we'll be better equipped to manage the hard times when they inevitably come our way.

Stronger together

Nonni rely on each other and often work in perfect synchronicity. Nonno might grow the tomatoes and nonna might preserve them. Nonna might weed the garden and nonno might plant the flowers. Nonna might watch Italian shows on TV while nonno does the crossword. Nonno might make the coffee and nonna will surely drink it! They are stronger together than they are apart and nonni form a perfect partnership. Find ways to create symbiotic workings with your partner. Nonnas tell us it's a really important way to keep a long-term relationship strong.

Family love

The thing that unites nonna and nonno more than anything is their shared love for their family. They love their children, they particularly love their grandchildren, they love their siblings, they love their friends. They are pretty united in love. And there is no stronger force than that! Love what your partner loves. Talk about your joint loves. A lot. Let the loves you share be one of the things that unites you.

TALES OF NONNA (AND NONNO!)

'My nonna and nonno were a funny pair. Nonno could be quite grumpy but he was mostly matter-of-fact and didn't suffer fools. He loved my nonna's cooking and was lucky enough to enjoy it for two meals a day for most of his life! But he was also her harshest critic. I remember one meal of homemade pasta where he told my nonna she hadn't salted the pasta water. She was adamant that she had. I couldn't taste whether the pasta had been cooked in salted water as the sauce was quite salty.'

'Nonna then looked at Nonno with a strange expression on her face, as though she was thinking deeply. Neither of them spoke. She then told him he was right. The phone had rung as she had put the water for the pasta on the stove and she had forgotten to salt the water. He replied, 'I told you.' And they both smiled at each other and nodded. I mean the meal was completely delicious but somehow Nonno found a way to fault it and Nonna almost seemed pleased. Maybe she was happy he paid such close attention. I have no idea. All I could think was that if someone criticised my cooking when I had worked so hard to make a delicious meal I'd kill them, not smile at them.' – J

Tante belle cose!

The literal translation of tante belle cose *is 'lots of beautiful things'. It's a wish and a blessing and is used the way English speakers use 'all the best' or 'best wishes'. Nonnas say it a lot!*

It's a heartfelt expression of love and goodwill. Try to offer genuine good wishes to the people in your life as much as you possibly can. We need to be inspired by the way nonnas are so happy for others.

The good life

What nonnas are really saying when they say *tante belle cose* is that they wish you get to enjoy the good things in life. Just the good things. And nonnas truly know what the good things are. They wish for you to have a life filled with love, laughter, adventure and really, really good food. They want you to be happy and have a meaningful and balanced life. They see the stresses and pressures of the modern world and they reject them; they don't want you to be worn down by the daily grind. The good life is one of fulfilment, where you know what's truly important. *Tante. Belle. Cose.*

A happy life

Nonnas truly wish for what's best for us. They genuinely want those they love to have a happy life. It's so simple and so sweet. Nonnas are very forward orientated and despite, or because of, the difficult lives they may have had they focus on the future rather than the past. And their loved ones, especially their family, are the future they care most about. Try to have a similar outlook. Spend more time thinking about your future than you do about your past.

The sweet life

As hard as life can be for a nonna, they still appreciate the sweet things in life, and no, not just biscotti. Dancing and singing are a big part of nonnas' lives and something they have enjoyed since they were small. Playing card games or tombola with friends is something they look forward to. Talking politics or gossiping with their siblings and friends is a joy, albeit a loud one. Think about the week that just passed. How much of it did you spend doing fun things with the people you love? Enough? Could you have carved out more time for the sweet things in life?

Hopes and dreams

Nonnas are very genuine in their good wishes. They have sacrificed so much for their children and grandchildren and they hope their family get to reap the benefits of those sacrifices. Some nonnas hope for academic success for their loved ones, while others focus on health and happiness. But no matter what their hopes and dreams actually are, they truly want what is best for those they love. Being genuinely happy for people and their successes, and wishing them the best, is a muscle you can exercise if it doesn't come naturally. Don't compare yourself to anyone and remember their success has nothing to do with yours. There's enough good fortune to go around.

START EACH DAY THE NONNA WAY

Nonnas don't tend to mess about in the mornings and they do what they need to in order to best greet the day ahead of them. Follow their example and:

Make your bed

Fold your pyjamas and put them under your pillow

Drink coffee

Water the plants

Shower and get dressed

ACQUA
di
ROSE

CHAPTER FOUR

~

LA BELLEZZA

Fare una passeggiata

Go. For. A. Walk. Nonnas instinctively know how good walking is for you so they do it every day.

They just get up and go. They walk in their communities. They walk in their town squares. They walk for exercise. They walk for a social outing. They walk for fresh air. They walk for their mental health. They walk in the countryside. They walk with friends. They walk alone. They just walk. Copy them in this! Nonnas know best.

Every single day

Go for a walk every single day. Build it into your day. If you're physically able, go outside and walk. One foot in front of the other. The cumulative benefits of regular walks are many and varied. Nonnas know that they might bump into a friend, they might just enjoy some fresh air and they might be better placed to spy on their neighbours. All sorts of things can happen when you're out on a walk that can't happen if you're at home watching TV or scrolling through your phone. Open yourself up to those possibilities. So much is happening on our own doorsteps and it's mostly the nonnas out there experiencing it.

Health benefits

The health benefits of regular walks, even just 30 minutes per day, are extensive: increased cardiovascular and pulmonary (heart and lung) fitness; reduced risk of heart disease and stroke; improved management of conditions such as high blood pressure, high cholesterol, joint and muscular pain and diabetes; stronger bones and improved balance. Walking is just really good for you. Nonnas may be pounding the pavement without being fully aware of these benefits, they just recognise that it makes them feel good to be out. You know about the health benefits so there is really no excuse for you not to be out there.

Mental-health benefits

Walking improves mood, self-esteem and sleep quality. It can also reduce stress, anxiety and fatigue. Physically active people have up to a 30 per cent reduced risk of becoming depressed, and staying active helps those who are depressed to recover. In older people, staying active can improve cognitive function, memory, attention and also processing speed, and reduce the risk of cognitive decline. Knowing all this, why wouldn't you go for a daily walk?

Nonna style

Some nonnas might be pushing up their heart rate and working up a sweat on their daily walks. Others might have a more relaxed meandering style. In Italy, nonnas can often be found walking around a piazza. Locals gather at the piazza on a regular basis. It's a place you're likely to see people you know, a place you can get a coffee or do some shopping, a place perfect for people watching, a place that is the very heart of where you live. See if you can find the equivalent in your local area. It might be a shopping centre or a strip of shops, it might be a park or community centre. Walk there and explore what's on your doorstep.

Women walking

It's not uncommon to see groups of nonnas going for a walk together and using the occasion as a social outlet. They will chat and catch up as they walk. It's a beautiful sight. Why don't you grab some friends for your next walk and do it nonna style?

27
volterracasa.it

50

RISOTTO MILANESE

You've been so virtuous with all that walking so surely you can now enjoy this classic and very easy to make risotto from Milano.

Ingredients

2 tbsp olive oil

1 small onion, finely diced

300g arborio, carnaroli or vialone nano rice

Pinch of saffron

1.2l chicken stock

70g parmesan, grated

40g unsalted butter

Salt

Serves four, or two hungry Italians

1. Heat the olive oil in a large heavy-based saucepan. Add the onion and cook until translucent. Add the rice and cook for a couple of minutes before adding the saffron.

2. Add a ladleful of stock and stir until the liquid is absorbed. Continue doing this until you have used all the stock and the rice is al dente but not crunchy.

3. Add the parmesan, butter and salt. The rice should have a creamy texture and be golden in colour.

Olive oil inside and out

In a world where we are constantly bombarded with new skincare products that promise to tone, lift, brighten and plump, the way of the nonnas can seem deceptively simple. But Nonna truly knows best. A nonna's beauty regime can seem a little unorthodox. Unlike many of us, Nonna doesn't apply thirteen different products to her skin and hair before she leaves the bathroom.

In fact, Nonna could probably whittle down her skin and hair care to one completely natural single-source ingredient: olive oil. It's an ingredient you should already have in your house, it's completely natural and there is no plastic waste. Are you ready to rethink your beauty regime?

Olive skin

There is a reason an Italian's skin tone is often called 'olive'. Nonna covers herself, her children and her grandchildren in the liquid gold daily. Dry hands? Put some coarse salt and olive oil in a dish and massage into your hands. Dandruff? Rub some olive oil into your scalp. Many a nonna drinks two to four tablespoons of olive oil per day for medicinal and digestive reasons – your gut microbes will love you for it (or at least that's what Nonna says). And almost every meal starts with a decent glug of olive oil going into the pan and is finished with a generous drizzle of extra virgin olive oil.

Eat and drink your oil

Nonnas have always recognised the value and place of olive oil in a balanced and healthy diet. The average Italian consumes more than 13 litres of olive oil per year – something we should all aspire to. Nonna cooks with extra virgin and regular olive oil. Extra virgin olive oil is saved for salad dressings and for drizzling on meals once they're cooked as it's the premium first pressing. Olive oil is used for simple dishes and for skincare. Nonna might make soap with it. She's likely to rub it on her skin and hair. The options are endless!

Il malocchio

Olive oil does have one more use: it can be used to remove the evil eye (*malocchio*). The evil eye is a curse transmitted by a person's eyes, believed to cause injury or bad luck to the person at whom it is directed. The most common cause of the evil eye is someone who is jealous. A nonna wanting to remove the *malocchio* takes a bowl of water and holds a spoonful of olive oil over it. She does the sign of the cross and offers a silent prayer. She then drops three to five drops of olive oil into the water with her little finger. This is repeated three times. If the oil disperses into the water then the evil eye is confirmed, if it floats and remains separate from the water then the evil eye has been broken.

There are other evil-eye preventatives including hanging garlic plaits in the house, throwing salt over your left shoulder and keeping horseshoes around your house. If you ever think someone is giving you the evil eye, ball your right hand into a fist and then point your index and little fingers. This is a horn or *corno* symbol and it ensures whatever bad thoughts are being sent your way go back to the person sending them. Some people may think that you're encouraging them to 'rock on'. Only nearby nonnas will know the truth and nod in approval.

Olive oil for breakfast

Italians are not big on breakfast as a concept. You'll rarely find muesli or cereal in an Italian household. If breakfast is eaten at home it might well be stale bread and bright green fresh extra virgin olive oil with salt sprinkled on top. Olive oil on bread is truly the breakfast of champions. And it's always eaten with an espresso of course.

So don't complicate your life with a 10-step beauty regime and a cupboard full of unhealthy saturated oils – turns out you only need one thing. Olive oil will keep you healthy inside and out, as well as keep you safe from the evil eye.

TALES OF NONNA

'When I was a baby my Nonna thought my skin wasn't olive enough. She worried I had the lighter complexion of a northern Italian so she rubbed my skin in olive oil and put me outside, butt naked, to crawl around in the sun on a very hot day. We now know a lot about UV rays and the fragile skin of a baby so this is definitely not recommended. I did however roast up like a chicken and Nonna was very happy with her handiwork. I also smelled delicious. But sometimes it turns out Nonna doesn't exactly know best.' – J

OLIVE OIL CAKE

The nonnas of Liguria have long used olive oil in their baking. They're known for simple, no-fuss baking that's completely delicious. And the best part is that because the cake uses olive oil rather than butter, it just gets better with time.

Ingredients

2 lemons, finely grate the zest and then juice (you'll need approximately 200ml of lemon juice)

325g caster sugar

3 eggs

300ml milk

300ml extra virgin olive oil

300g plain flour

1 tbsp baking powder

Pinch of salt

1. Preheat oven to 180°C. Butter and line a 23cm round tin.
2. In a large bowl, rub the zest and sugar together until the sugar is moist and smells amazing.
3. Beat the eggs and the lemony sugar until pale and thick. Add the milk, olive oil and lemon juice and combine.
4. In a separate bowl, sift the flour, baking powder and salt and make a well. Slowly add the wet ingredients to the flour, mixing until just blended. Pour mixture into your cake tin.
5. Bake for 40 minutes. Test to see if a skewer comes out clean. If it does the cake is ready. If it doesn't, bake for another 10 minutes and check again.
6. Once cooked, allow the cake to cool in the tin for 15 minutes before turning out to cool completely, then serve.

Dress up to go out

No nonna would be seen outside of the house in anything but her finest threads. She'll be looking nonna chic whenever she leaves her home. While at home she will be quite casual with her hair in rollers, a housedress with an apron over it, and a pair of old shoes or sandals on her feet.

Nonna knows how to be comfortable at home but she wouldn't dream of wearing what she wears at home outside of the house. Nonnas dress up to go out almost without exception. Try to think about your clothes as 'home clothes' and 'out clothes'. It will mean you're always comfortable when you're at home and you always look your best when you're out in the world.

Sunday best

Nonnas save their finest clothes for Sundays. Sundays loom large for many Italian households with mass and often a family lunch. On these and other religious days, Nonna busts out her best outfits. She dresses to impress. Give this a try. Change out of your good clothes when you get home. Never cook without wearing an apron. Save your best clothes for special events.

Home is for the housedress

But Nonna knows that not every day is Sunday. Sometimes you just want to wear comfy clothes and that's what she does. Nonna's chic housedress style is hard to replicate but she looks fab and is ready for anything – gardening, washing, dancing to the Italian radio, watching TV. The nonna housedress is incredibly versatile and means you're not putting your good clothes through their paces when you're at home. This keeps them nonna nice for when you step out. Owning a housedress is incredibly liberating. It's the dress you can relax in and cook, clean, garden, anything! It doesn't matter if it gets dirty, or even tears – you're only wearing it at home.

Homemade and mended

Many nonnas grew up at a time when clothes were often homemade. Many nonnas can at least mend their own clothes. They buy good quality clothing and wouldn't know what fast fashion is. If clothes require mending, they do it themselves. Their clothes last them a lifetime, literally. So take a silk scarf from Nonna's wardrobe and focus on buying well-made classic pieces of clothing and accessories. Buy the best quality you can find (this doesn't always mean the most expensive, but cost can be a limiting factor). Take care of the clothes you have and learn to mend them. Polish your shoes and bags regularly. Hang your clothes up immediately after wearing them. Dry clean your winter coats at the end of the season and hang them in plastic sheets. Annually replace lavender and bay-leaf sachets in your closet to deter moths. Resole shoes that are getting a bit tired. Handwash as much as possible – it's so much gentler than a washing machine – and dry clothes, especially woolens, flat. Take care of, and pride in, your stuff and you'll find it looks better and lasts longer.

Don't wash too often

Nonnas do not wash their clothes every time they wear them. In fact, they rarely wash them. Nonnas are the best-smelling women around so don't for a second think they stink. So, what's their secret? Firstly, Nonnas focus on keeping themselves clean though they shower less often than we do. It's common for an Italian house to have a bidet and Nonnas use it regularly to clean intimate areas, and they clean their upper bodies with a face washer. Nonnas want to keep their natural oils (plus the olive oil they add) on their skin and don't want to be washing it away. They also regularly air their clothes outside or in the bathroom rather than washing them. Nonnas grew up at a time when washing machines were rare so their instinct is to reduce washing. They also know that good-quality clothing does not need regular washing, an airing will do. It also means their clothes last longer and colours fade less. So before you throw everything in the washing basket, take a nonna minute to consider whether you could hold off.

Nonnas in black

In many parts of Italy it has been traditional for widows to wear black for twelve months after their husband dies. It's seen as a sign of mourning. Many Italian nonnas are no longer following this custom but it's not unusual to see a nonna rocking it in black – not because she's a hipster but because her culture encourages her to show her grief publicly. At the end of the twelve months, Nonna can return to wearing colourful clothes to mark the end of the official mourning period. Italians celebrate life with gusto. Death is treated with dignity and an element of practicality, but grief is felt deeply. Most mourners at an Italian funeral would be dressed in all black even today. Graves are carefully tended by the family of the deceased and visiting the graves of loved ones is a regular occurrence, especially on religious days.

NO QUESTION IS TOO PRIVATE

For nonnas, nothing is too personal. They're happy to ask about anything and the thing is, they're not shaming, just reporting on what they see and asking what they want to know. Here is a list of actual questions asked by actual nonnas:

**You look fat.
How much weight
you put on?**

**You look skinny.
Why you no eating?**

**You old now.
When you get
married?**

**This boy, he love
you? So when you
get married?**

**You old now.
When you have
babies?**

**When I your age
I have two babies.
When you have
babies?**

**You have two babies.
You need another one,
yes?**

CHAPTER FIVE

~

THE NONNA APPROACH

Auguri!

The word 'auguri' has no single translation. It can be used to mean 'well wishes', 'congratulations' and 'happy birthday'. Nonnas are very good celebrators. They will take advantage of any milestone and use it as a reason to get the family together.

Birthdays, anniversaries, religious holidays, graduations, seasonal occasions, nonnas are the first ones to suggest a party. Celebrations generally contain all the things nonnas like: family, friends, food, fun, prosecco, dancing. It can be easy to let milestones pass by in our busy lives but nonnas remind us of the importance of taking the time to celebrate the good things. It's all part of living *la dolce vita*. The sweet life means a life spent celebrating special moments and making memories.

Gioia (Joy)

Italians tend to be highly expressive of joy and happiness, both vocally and physically with frequent use of gestures and touch. Nonnas are not afraid to show their joy. A nonna at her grandchild's wedding is the happiest woman on earth. So next time you or someone you loves gets a promotion or has an upcoming birthday, throw a party and celebrate the joy!

Feasts

Too often we feel overwhelmed by the idea of feeding a large group of people. Most nonnas don't know that feeling. They get a rush of adrenaline. But you don't need to be a hardcore nonna to prepare an impressive feast for your friends and family; cooking doesn't have to be complicated. You can make simple food or even just make large antipasto platters for everyone to graze on. Nonnas use special occasions as an excuse so they can provide a feast for those they love. You can, too!

The more the merrier

Nonnas will never cap the numbers at an event. Being generous and giving is good for the soul. For them, it's very much the more the merrier. They can always make more food, get more chairs, squeeze in at the table. They want celebrations to be big, joyous and delightful for all. And we should follow their lead. It's easier than you think to add more people to an event you're already planning. And it's definitely true that the more, the merrier.

Making memories

Memories don't make themselves and nonnas understand the importance of marking occasions and thereby creating memories. These celebrations are a great way to bring people together on a regular basis so that life doesn't get in the way of strong connections. Nonnas often sit back and watch, they love seeing other people chatting and enjoying each other's company. They're not forcing connections actively, they're simply giving their family and friends many and repeated instances where they are in the same room. What an incredible role to play. You too can be that person. Bring people together and sit back and enjoy.

Presents

Nonnas are often very good gift givers. They listen carefully to what you say and observe your reactions to things. Many nonnas will give you anything you show an interest in. But nonnas are also aware that their presence is a kind of present and part of their desire to share celebratory moments is their belief that being together is the most important thing.

TALES OF NONNA

'My nonna made lasagna for the lunch at my Communion. She arrived early in the morning with four huge oven trays heavy with lasagna. I don't remember much from that day but the smell of lasagna wafting through the house as I traipsed around in my cute white dress is the strongest memory. What I would give to have just one more piece of her lasagna!' – J

FEAST IDEAS

Putting feasts together takes a little thought about what goes with what. Here are some menu ideas for various situations:

A Sunday lunch: prosciutto wrapped around rockmelon, risotto Milanese, cotolette with roast potatoes and peas, cannoli

Very special occasion: antipasto, lasagna, roast meats and vegetables, tiramisu

Simple dinner with friends: marinated olives and artichokes, roast chicken with lemon and potatoes, olive oil cake

Spontaneous quick dinner: toasted bread rubbed with garlic cloves and olive oil, spaghetti puttanesca, ice cream with olive oil and salt

Date night: roasted capsicum bruschetta, spaghetti cacio e pepe, peaches in prosecco

Gesticulate (and sing and laugh and dance)

Nonnas do not hide how they feel. Outward bursts of emotion are common. Hands fly wildly as Nonna makes her point. She throws her head back laughing. She hums a favourite song from her youth. She spontaneously starts dancing.

Nonnas express themselves boldly and loudly and with plenty of colour, panache and style. Think about the ways you communicate. Can you be more overt, more flamboyant, more colourful? If there's room for you to welcome nonna-style gesticulation and expressions of joy, give it a try!

Hand gestures

Most Italians can communicate as much with their hands as they do with their words and nonnas are the experts. Nonna can make it very clear how she's feeling with a simple hand gesture. For example, if she were to pretend bite her index finger while her hand is flat it means you're in pretty big trouble and you're driving her crazy. Start using your hands in your everyday communication. See if you're able to better communicate with those around you if you throw in some gesticulation.

Canta, canta!

Many nonnas love to sing. Singing is often incorporated into everyday chores. Nonna is shelling peas and singing? Nonna is rolling pasta and singing? Nonna is pruning the plum tree and singing? You bet she is. Nonna enjoys singing and there is no stopping her. It's an expression of joy for her. It helps pass the time and makes an otherwise repetitive task fun. Nonna really has the right idea here. Next time you're working on a boring task (spreadsheets come to mind) sing one of your favourite songs aloud. The song itself shouldn't actually be playing. Just belt it out. Feels pretty good, right?

Laugh it out

Nonna is not afraid to lol. And I mean actually laugh out loud, not just say lol (Nonna would never say lol). She might laugh easily or you might have to tease a laugh out of her, but either way laughing is part of the nonna way of life. Nonnas freely show their happiness without feeling self-conscious. These long-lived women are not easily embarrassed and when they feel joy, they want to show it. And that is a beautiful and powerful thing. Let yourself laugh freely and easily. If something tickles your funny bone throw your head back and let it out. Nonnas show us how to live boldly and we need to grab on to their apron strings and follow their lead with our hearts as open as theirs.

Swearing

Swearing in Italian is a lot of fun and quite a creative pursuit. Some nonnas are very happy to swear and they often come up with quite hilarious ways of doing it. They swear in exasperation of course, but they also sometimes swear out of happiness and silliness. Give it a try. Go on, swear like a nonna (see pages 254-255 for some examples). Be sure to use hand gestures while doing it for a full nonna dramatic effect.

Dance

Nonnas love to dance. It's quite common for nonnas to go dancing at their local Italian community club. Nonnas also love to bust moves at their very favourite family events – weddings! They don't wait for someone to invite them onto the dance floor, nonnas just get up and boogie. Try to leave your inhibitions and hang-ups with the *bomboniere* (sugared almonds placed on the table at every Italian wedding ever) and dance if you feel like dancing. Forget about the 'dance like nobody is watching' thing. Heck, nonnas want people to watch them bust a move. Why wouldn't they! They look so cool up there. Nonnas enjoy a freedom and lack of self-consciousness that is truly impressive. Here are women who have lived and suffered and endured and enjoyed and loved and they want to show it.

GUIDE TO ITALIAN HAND GESTURES

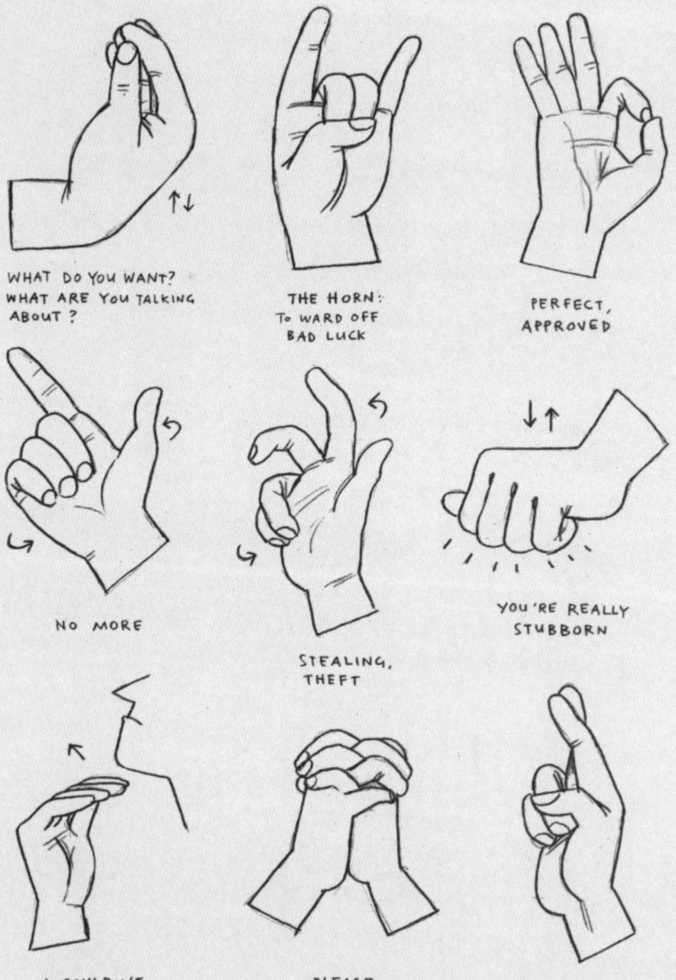
WHAT DO YOU WANT?
WHAT ARE YOU TALKING ABOUT?
THE HORN:
TO WARD OFF BAD LUCK
PERFECT,
APPROVED
NO MORE
STEALING,
THEFT
YOU'RE REALLY
STUBBORN
I COULDN'T
CARE LESS
PLEASE,
I BEG YOU
FINGERS CROSSED,
GOOD LUCK!

NONNA-APPROVED SWEAR WORDS

These are very gentle Italian swear words that nonna would be okay with:

Che cavolo
literally means 'what a cabbage' but 'cabbage' is standing in for another Italian swear word that sounds similar but is much ruder.

Stronzino/a
used to tell someone they are being annoying or a jerk.

Accidenti!

a gentle way to say 'damn' or 'that sucks'.

Porca miseria

literally 'pork poverty' but used to mean 'for goodness sake'.

Che palle

literally 'what balls' and used to mean 'what the hell' or 'how annoying/ boring'.

R

TORANTE
Take Coffee

TALES OF NONNA

'When one of my cousins got married, Nonna asked me to take her outfit shopping. We went to so many shops and she tried on so many outfits – always a matching skirt and top with a bit of bling. She loved her bling. Every time she came out of the dressing room she practised dancing in her outfit. Every time!'

'She tried on at least 40 different outfits that day and the only thing she seemed to care about was that she could dance in it. I laugh now but it was a long day and by the end I couldn't take it anymore. Finally, she found an outfit she liked and danced in it for a while before I took her home. I'll never forget my cousin's wedding – Nonna danced the whole night. Her smile lit up the dance floor.' – T

Riposo

After all that dancing and singing, nonnas usually need a riposo *(rest). And they are surprisingly very good at resting. In Italy it's common to have a nap after lunch, the biggest meal of the day.*

This reviving nap takes place during the hottest part of the day when it's best to be inside avoiding the heat. Nonnas also take the time to put their feet up and watch their favourite TV shows or play cards. So they work hard, they play hard and they rest hard. If you're already a napper then you're all set but if you're one of those people who doesn't typically nap then this is for you.

Nap time

A nap at lunchtime can be incredibly restorative and will set you up for a very productive afternoon and evening. In Italy many stores and businesses close for several hours in the middle of the day. This allows employees to go home, have lunch with their families and have a rest before returning to work in the afternoon. If you have any flexibility in your working life, give it a try! Simply eat a big bowl of pasta for lunch, tidy up the dishes and head to bed for about 45 minutes. You'll wake up feeling revived and raring to go! There's a reason why Italians swear by the *riposo*.

Adapted for today

If a lunchtime extended break is not possible, the modern equivalent might be finishing early every second Friday during the summer months. This allows people the opportunity to take some time for themselves where they could take a nap, get their hair done, spend time with their families or just do anything they like! Should you have the power to make this happen at your workplace, all studies, including those done by governments, research institutes and businesses, show initiatives like this make staff happier and more productive. Nonnas don't need a study to know this, of course. They always know what's best.

Forget the economy

The Italian *riposo* is not evidently good for business. Tourists are often shocked to find businesses, especially ones that offer services to tourists, closed at what they consider to be peak times of the busy day. What is greatest about the *riposo* is its resilience. Economic forces can't eradicate it. Despite what might be best in economic terms, businesses shut up shop and people head home for two things very important to Italians: food and forty winks. Resting is just that important. So is eating but we've well and truly covered that.

Not just a nap

It is important to note that the Italian *riposo* is not just nap time. People cook and eat lunch, do the dishes, spend time together and have a little rest. They're not just napping for the three or four hours businesses close. The *riposo* and its resilience is without doubt connected to the Italian concept of *dolce far niente*. Incorporating rest and relaxation into daily life is important to Italians and especially to nonnas. They want to nourish those they love with food and with an approach to life that's healthy and balanced.

Digestion

It's gospel to nonnas that a nap aids digestion and is an important part of the eating experience. The weird thing is that after a huge meal of Nonna's deliciousness, a nap seems like the only sensible thing. Upon waking up you might just find that you do have room for one more serve of cannelloni. It's weird but true that even after a short nap you can fit in some more food. Or at least a coffee and biscotto.

The best time

If you've spent any time in Italy you may have learnt that what makes the *riposo* so great is that you get to spend time with those you love at the best time of the day. You're a better you at midday than you are at 7pm stumbling home after a long continuous work day. The sun is up, the breeze is refreshing, your spirit is in good shape. It's not just about spending time together it's about the quality of the time you spend together. It's so easy to feel tired and worn down at the end of a long day. By breaking the day up, Italians are allowing people to be with those they love at the best time of day.

Quality of life

The *riposo* is all about adding quality to life. Italians will sacrifice economic gains for lifestyle ones. How many of us can say that? Are you willing to consider your life in terms of quality and make decisions that improve the very essence of your life, decisions that are perhaps to the detriment of your finances? Italians do exactly that every single day.

DON'T FIGHT IT

If you're visiting Italy and finding the riposo *hours drive you crazy, the key is not to fight it. Do what the locals do and use the time to relax. Actually relax. Find a tree and sit under it. Eat the food and drink the local wine that you bought before the shops closed at midday. Lie down. Take off your shoes. Close your eyes. Do you see? That's what the* riposo *is all about. Rest. We all need it, it's just that the Italians, particularly the* nonnas*, take it seriously.*

BE MORE NONNA

10 easy steps

In everything you do in life, try to be more nonna. Incorporate a nonna-approved approach and you'll find that life is bolder, better and simpler. These women know what they're doing.

1.

Shop local more often

Many nonnas shop for food locally and regularly. They want the freshest possible ingredients and make time to get them almost every day. Instead of doing one big shop each week, keep your pantry well stocked and pop by the shops on your way home for the freshest ingredients. Nonnas also shop seasonally and wouldn't be interested in fruit or vegetables outside of their season for two main reasons: they're not at their best and they're more expensive. Smart nonnas.

2.

Grow your own

Many nonnas are excellent gardeners and grow delicious fruits and vegetables and show-stopping flowers. They connect with the earth and the seasons and use gardening as an outlet to get outside and get their hands dirty. Start growing something. It can be as simple as planting a lemon tree in an old wine barrel. Or 20 garlic bulbs in a small patch of garden (remember, 20 cloves of garlic will give you 20 heads of garlic!). Or scattering some parsley seeds so you never have to buy this incredibly generous and easy-to-grow herb again. Start simple and small. The key to gardening is consistency, so don't bite off more than you can chew when you first start.

3.

Take care of your stuff

There is many a nonna out there with plastic on her couch. She wants to keep it nice so she wraps it in plastic and basically only lets special guests sit on it. While this might be one instance where Nonna isn't leading the way environmentally, there is something to be said for taking care of your stuff. Nonnas keep their clothes and homewares in excellent condition. Nonna's stove might look brand new despite being forty years old. Take care of your stuff and it will last for a lifetime.

4.

Stand up for yourself

Nonnas take no crap. If you try to push in front of them at the deli they will give you a serve. They are old and bold and refuse to back down. Bring a little nonna attitude to your daily life. Stand tall (even if you're 5 foot 1). Bring some Italian in and start with, 'Mi scusi, but I think you'll find I was next,' and then proceed to ask for what you want. Nonnas aren't always nice.

5.
Gossip with friends

Nonnas are sweet women who love to gossip. They *love* to gossip. It seems to give them life. As a general approach, gossiping is not a great way to spend your time and energy, but nonnas seem to derive vigour from it, so who am I to judge? Nonnas also seem able to find ways to gossip kindly. They're not malicious so much as crazily curious. If you want a nonna to keep something to herself simply say *acqua in bocca*. It literally means 'water in your mouth' and is a way to ask someone to keep something private. It may not always work with nonnas but it's worth a try.

6.
Be more social

Nonnas love to socialise and generally prefer not to be alone. They will meet friends for a morning or afternoon coffee (espresso style) and will always prefer to eat a meal with family. So put your phone down and gather your people together. Spending time with family and friends is so important and yet when we let life get busy it's often the first thing we push to the side.

7.
Be cheeky

Nonnas are funny and a little bit cheeky. They like to laugh and to make people laugh. Many nonnas get a special glint in their eye when their cheeky side takes over. These fun-loving women know what's important in life and what's not.

8.
Keep it simple

Find the simplicity in everything and notice its beauty. Nonnas do not overcomplicate their lives. They believe in the basics – you can make pasta from flour and water, save last year's seeds for this year's crop, buy quality clothes that will last. Life needn't be complicated.

9.

Seek spirituality

Many nonnas are deeply religious and take great comfort in their faith. They see themselves as a small part of God's larger plan. This sense of perspective allows them to recognise that they are but a speck of dust in the larger cosmos and helps them not to get too self-absorbed or self-obsessed – something we can all work at. Try to remember that everything is connected and we as individuals are of minor importance in the bigger picture. Don't get too obsessed with the self and try to think about the greater good.

10.

Let love be your guide

The main way you can increase your nonna vibes is to let love guide you through life. Imbue everything you do with love. Food will taste better, relationships will be more meaningful, work will be more satisfying. If love (nonna style of course) is your guiding principle, you can't go too far wrong.

The nonna manifesto

Nonna has guided her family through many ups and downs. She has weathered many storms and has enjoyed many sunny afternoons. She has done it all with love; unconditional and all-encompassing. If you truly want to live a bolder and more nonna-like existence, then all you need to do is follow the nonna manifesto.

What would Nonna do?

Should you find yourself in a situation where you don't know what to do, just ask: What would Nonna do? Would she take the shortcut or would she do it properly? Would she hold back or would she go in boldly? Would she care what other people thought or would she be fearless? These four words will save you so much time and angst. Once you can think like a nonna you can live like one and that will make all the difference.

Be bold

Nonnas, even the shy and quietly spoken ones, are usually bold. They have opinions and they feel things strongly. They know how to get things done. They don't suffer fools. Life isn't about coziness, restraint and minimalism, it's about living with conviction and courage. Nonnas teach us so many things, but what they embody, in everything they do and how they do it, is courage. These women hold up the sky.

Love

A nonna's love is so deep and unconditional. She just loves you. So much! If you're lucky enough to have known a nonna's love then let that be her legacy and love how she loved you. What a thing to inherit! If you haven't known a nonna's love yourself then take a deep breath and feel your lungs expand. Now imagine doing the same thing with your heart. Expand it. That's the only way to love like a nonna. Work that muscle and every time you can, choose to show love in big ways. The muscle will grow and expand until you're loving deeply, passionately and with reckless abandon. Feels pretty amazing, right?

The importance of food

Never underestimate the importance of food. Use it to nurture your friends and family and show them love. Work hard on perfecting a few dishes – cooking a few dishes well will set you up for the rest of your life. If you're able, try to grow some of your own food. Herbs are a very easy place to start, but garlic is also easy and can be grown in any size garden. Plaited garlic lasts for about 10 months so you can grow enough to last you almost a full year. And if you're anything like Nonna, you use garlic in every single dish!

Beauty in simplicity

Nonnas keep things pretty simple. From their single-ingredient beauty regime to cooking by first principles to caring for and mending the clothes they wear for life, they do not covet stuff. They have and use what they need, and apart from having a *caffettiera* in every cup size, they keep things pretty simple. And there is such beauty in simplicity. It's truly where the magic is.

Nonnas never retire

Once a nonna, you're a nonna for life. There is no retirement plan. She embodies her nonna approach to life forever. Pick the elements of a nonna's guide to life that resonate best with you and embrace them fully. Carry them with you for the rest of your days.

Nonna knows best

There is nothing more special than a nonna. She represents love and courage. She cares for her family more than anything else in the world. She wants to feed people more than any person should eat in one sitting. She is kind, she is strong, she is nonna.

In conclusion ...

The influence nonnas have on their families cannot be overstated. I am who I am because of my nonnas, Paolina and Vincenzina. These women taught me how to cook, they taught me how to garden, they taught me how to stick up for myself, they taught me how to play cards, they taught me how to move through the world. Nonna Paolina spent hours teaching me how to cut the flesh off green olives so I could stuff them with minced meats and crumb and deep fry them to make a dish from our hometown Ascoli Piceno. I was initially terrible at this and left most of the flesh on the pip. She just kept showing me until I finally got it and stopped wasting all those precious olives!

Nonna Vincenzina taught me a faster way to shell peas so we could get through the huge crop she grew. The fact that I ate as many raw as I bagged to be frozen never got me in trouble. Whenever I think of my nonnas the first thing I think of is love. The love that they gave me even when I refused to speak to them in Italian, even when I was an awful teenager. These women loved me and taught me and cared for me. I cannot think of better teachers of life and love than my nonnas. They showed me how to live a meaningful life and maybe now they've shown you, too.

Image credits

p.4 Andrew Stewardson
p.6 Viola Damiani
p.10-11 La So/Unsplash
p.15 Quaid Lagan/Unsplash
p.30-31 Sven Johanson/Unsplash
p.41 Lindsay Lenard/Unsplash
p.52-53 Laura Seidlitz/Unsplash
p.63 Wolfgang Hassel Mann/Unsplash
p.66-67 Liubov Ilchuk/Unsplash
p.76-77 Anita Austvika/Unsplash
p.81 Ava Sol/Unsplash
p.88-89 Reka Biro Horvath/Unsplash
p.100-101 Alexiaa Sim/Unsplash
p.107 Guiseppe Mondi/Unsplash
p.113 RedCharlie/Unsplash
p.119 Anna Auza/Unsplash
p.131 Cristian Newman/Unsplash
p.134-135 Nathalie Jolie/Unsplash
p.141 Chris Holgersson/Unsplash

p.146-147 Milada Vigerova/Unsplash
p.156-157 Ingo Hamm/Unsplash
p.161 Skiathos Greece/Unsplash
p.169 Rod Long/Unsplash
p.175 Joyce Huis/Unsplash
p.178-179 Edi Libedinsky/Unsplash
p.182-183 Hiral Patel/Unsplash
p.189 Cristina Gottardi/Unsplash
p.192-193 Juliana Malta/Unsplash
p.207 Cristina Gottardi/Unsplash
p.208-209 Alisa Anton/Unsplash
p.217 Roberta Sorge/Unsplash
p.222-223 Nazar Hrabovyi/Unsplash
p.230-231 Katy Cao/Unsplash
p.239 Vincent Rivaud
p.256-257 Kati Smetherman/Unsplash
p.268-269 Davide Cantelli/Unsplash
p.281 Cristian Newman/Unsplash
p.284-285 Anastasia Zhenin/Unsplash

First published by Affirm Press in 2020
a Simon & Schuster (Australia) Pty Limited company
Wurundjeri Woiwurrung Country
Level 3, 162 Collins Street Melbourne VIC 3000

Affirm Press is located on the unceded land of the Wurundjeri Woiwurrung peoples of the Kulin Nation. Affirm Press pays respect to their Elders past and present.

10 11 12 13 14

ISBN: 9781925972627 (hardback)

A catalogue record for this book is available from the National Library of Australia

Cover and internal design by Emily Thiang
Typeset in Charter 11/13pt
Printed and bound in China by C&C Offset Printing Co., Ltd.